How To Write and Publish Non-Fiction

a Self-Publishing Guide for First-Time Writers

Kenn Crawford

CRAWFORD HOUSE PUBLISHING

Grand Lake Road, Nova Scotia, Canada B1M 1A1

Copyright © 2021 Crawford House Publishing

Written by Kenn Crawford
Cover Design by Luke Romyn

ABOUT THE AUTHOR

Born in Toronto in 1966, Kenn Crawford grew up in the coal-mining town of Glace Bay on Cape Breton, an island off the coast of Nova Scotia, Canada.

He spent his childhood reading books and making up stories; a hobby that led to his love of writing poetry, songs, and short stories. Eventually, he began writing books and screenplays.

In 2002, he wrote a weekly newspaper column about songwriting and home recording. He appeared in *The Cape Bretoner Magazine* as the featured songwriter, he founded one of the largest online groups for home recording enthusiasts, and he founded the official online mailing list for amateur and professional ventriloquists.

In 2016, he took his love of making up stories to the next level by writing, shooting, and directing short films.

In 2018, he won a "Canada Shorts" Director's Award of Commendation.

Over the years he has founded several businesses, including an advertising company, a computer store, and a restaurant, all of which he later sold to pursue other business ventures. He also worked as a disc jockey, ventriloquist, musician, and owned a small recording studio.

Kenn lives on Cape Breton Island with his fiancé, Margie, shooting short films and music videos, and teaching writing and filmmaking workshops. He is currently working on several new fiction and nonfiction books.

For more information about Kenn, his writing and his film work, visit his website at: **www.kenncrawford.com**

OTHER BOOKS BY KENN CRAWFORD

FICTION

Dead Hunt: Some Things are Better Left Dead
(zombie thriller)

Code 900: A Derrick Stone Crime Story *(thriller)*

The Saga of Bayou Billy *(comedy)*

The Misadventures of Mallory Malo: A Ghost Story She's Dying to Tell You *(middle-grade)*

The Princess Knights *(children's story, young reader)*

NONFICTION

The Covid Chronicles:
Personal Pandemic Stories from Around the World: 2020
(true stories, memoirs, poems)

How to Write & Publish Non-Fiction: *a Self-Publishing Guide for First-Time Writers (Self-Help, DIY)*

FILM MAKING BOOKS

The Indie Filmmaker's Shot List: Create film and video shot lists *(200 pages - 8.5" x 11")*

The Indie Filmmaker's Storyboard Book: Create storyboards for your indie film or video shoot.
(200 pages - 8.5" x 11")

JOURNALS

Did I Roll My Eyes Out Loud? A Gratitude Journal for Pissed Off Women

The Five-Minute Gratitude Book for Kids: A Journal to Teach Children to Practice Being Grateful

For more information, visit: kenncrawford.com/books

To everyone who asked me how to write books,

Who hold a desire in their heart to write,

But are not sure how to get started…

This one is for you!

What's Inside

"It's none of their business that you have to learn how to write. Let them think you were born that way."

~ Ernest Hemingway

Part 1 – Why You Should Write a Book

If you are a business owner, thinking about starting a business, or you wish to advance your position in your current job, one of the best things you can do to help you grow your brand and position yourself as an authority figure in your niche is to write a book *(we will cover 'niche' in more detail shortly.)*

Some people want to 'give back' and 'pay it forward' as a thank you to all the people who directly and indirectly helped them over the years. If this sounds like you, one of the best ways to do that is by writing a book because not only can you help people in different states, provinces, or countries, but you can help a lot more of them with a book than you ever could by just helping the ones who come to you directly with a problem they need solving.

Writing and publishing a book carries a lot of weight because it's not every day that employers or the average person have the opportunity to talk with a published author.

"But Kenn, anybody can self-publish a book these days; it doesn't really mean much."

I've heard that before; my answer is always the same…

With today's technology, self-publishing, or indie publishing as it is more commonly referred, does make it a lot easier for anyone *to* publish a book, but here's the thing…

<u>Not that many people actually do</u> - they *dream* about it; they *say* they want to; but they *don't actually do it.*

According to one post I read by *The Synergy Whisperer*, 97% of people who start to write a book never finish it. I have read many blogs and watched countless videos on writing and indie book publishing who stated that anywhere from 95% to as high as 99% of author hopefuls fail to actually finish their book.

Why is that?

If modern technology and services like Amazon KDP (Kindle Direct Publishing) make publishing books that much easier, why aren't more people doing it?

Here's the cold, hard truth…

Many people <u>*want*</u> to write a book, some even <u>*start*</u> to write it, but only a small handful <u>*actually finish it*</u> because most of them jumped into writing not knowing what to expect, and sadly, the vast majority of them gave up when the novelty of *'being a writer'* wore off.

Maybe it was because it was more difficult than they thought, they didn't actually know what they were doing, or they were simply too impatient and quit because it didn't happen overnight. Regardless of their reasons, most people just give up!

This is why having your own book, even one that is self-published, still holds so much power and establishes you as a credible authority in your niche, because you succeeded where so many others have failed, and that is exactly why I wrote this guide... to help you succeed so you're not just another wannabe writer who kinda-sorta tried but gave up when the going got tough.

I want you to be the exception to the rule and finish your book.

WHAT EXACTLY IS A NICHE?

A niche can be described as a specialized segment of the market for a particular kind of product or service. A business niche is a specialized or focused area of a larger, broader market that businesses can serve to differentiate themselves from the competition. Business owners often try to find a niche in their industry that has underserved or unmet needs, and then serve and meet those needs so that their business will grow by being recognized as an authority in that niche.

For example, 'Pets' is an exceptionally large market because there is such a wide variety of pets and pet owners, making it a rather broad and unfocused market.

'Dogs' are a smaller niche because it excludes cats, birds, fish, snakes, lizards and so on. A specific breed of dog, such as a Pitbull, is an even smaller niche because that market is only for owners of pitbulls, not other dog breeds.

'Training Pitbulls' is a smaller niche within it because it excludes certain types of products and services such as dog food or breeding Pitbulls.

But even the 'Training Pitbulls" niche could be broken down further *(aka niched down or drilled down)* to only serve the needs of your country, state, or even just your city or hometown. Or you could niche down to serve female owners of Pitbulls, or female millennials who own Pitbulls, and so on.

Niching down is often recommended because you can better establish yourself as an expert which widens your sales opportunities because you specialize in that specific niche for a specialized audience (market), **but you can go overboard and drill down too far which actually limits your sales opportunities because now the market is too small.**

An example of a "too niched down market" would be writing a book for six-foot-tall, tattooed, Christian, female millennials who live in the suburbs of Boston who own three-legged, albino Pitbulls who are rescue dogs. You may think your laser-focused, super-niched-down market is underserved (and it most likely is) but **there are simply not enough people in that Super-Niched-Down Market to make writing a book specifically for them worthwhile.**

Or you can just write whatever book you want to write regardless if there is a market for it or not; just don't be surprised if your too-niched-down book doesn't sell very well.

For a business that offers specific services, such as in-person training, you would want to narrow down your niche a lot to attract specific clientele; there is no point in marketing your in-person training to people who live on the other side of the country, or in a different country altogether because they cannot attend your training.

As an author you don't want to only sell your book to the people in your hometown or state unless it is about something specific and unique to your town or state. Your goal is to write about a niche that attracts readers on a larger, possibly global scale, so as not to limit your book's selling potential.

Book sales is a numbers game… the more people who can benefit from your book the better. Just remember that a book that tries to appeal to everyone could end up being too broad, which doesn't really help people because there's not enough relevant information.

For example, an all-encompassing book with sections on learning how to play guitar, piano, drums, bass, violin, saxophone, and several other instruments probably wouldn't have much appeal because the vast majority of people do not have the desire to play, or even own, that many different instruments.

Not to mention, an all-encompassing book like that would only have a small section on playing each individual instrument, and you couldn't possibly cover enough relevant information in those smaller sections to make such a book worthwhile to anyone.

If you can play six different instruments, a one-size-fits-all 'How to' book like that will not sell very well because it would only be of interest to people who want to play those same six instruments, whereas six different books that focus on each individual instrument will sell much better because each book fills a specific niche.

Remember, book sales is a numbers game - the more books you have, the more money you earn, it really is that simple, but it comes with one very important caveat:

Your book must provide readers with real value.

A book that is 'slapped together' in a few days of speed writing cannot provide much value because you did not put enough time and effort into creating the book. And yes, I have seen and read a few books on how to write and publish a book in as little as seven days. Most of those books suggested a lot of 'short cuts' that I do not recommend because the end result will always be a less than stellar book.

You can fool some of the people some of the time, but eventually, publishing shoddy books will come back to haunt you and ruin your reputation as a writer.

It is no coincidence that the majority of the *"book a week"* books that I have read also suggested creating fake author names for each book.

Why?

Because they know that if you keep publishing crappy books under the same name, your sales won't be all that great because once the reader discovers they wasted their hard-earned money on your crappy book, they will never buy another book from you again.

At the end of the day, it all boils down to this one, simple truth:

If you don't care about your book, no one else will either.

Your goal should never be to write and publish as many books as quickly as possible to make a quick buck. **Your goal as a writer should always be to produce your best work.**

You cannot build your brand and become an authority figure in your niche when you try to short cut your way to book publishing success - some things just take time. **Give your book the attention it deserves.**

HOW LONG DOES IT TAKE TO WRITE A BOOK?

There are too many variables to answer that specifically because writing is very personal, and includes a variety of factors such as:

- How much knowledge you have about your niche topic
- How fast you write (and type)
- How much (if any) research is needed
- How many hours per day you dedicate to your book
- How long it takes to proofread and edit it
- How quickly your beta readers can get back to you, and how long it takes to implement changes if needed
- How long it takes your editor (if you hired one)
- How long it takes you or someone else to create the cover
- The length of your book

There is no 'one-size-fits-all' answer when it comes to how long it will take you to write and publish your book. When all is said and done, **it takes as long as it takes**.

The more dedicated time you can spend working on your book, the better it will be, and the quicker you will be able to publish it. Speed should be the least of your worries; focus on writing and publishing a book you will be proud to put your name on.

The goal of this guide is to help you speed up the writing process as much as possible without sacrificing quality.

If you are looking for a *'Get Rich Quick'* method to writing and publishing success, this book is probably not for you. We'll cover what this book is, and what it's not, in the next section.

Don't be misled into believing you can write a high-quality book in just a few short days. You can't. As my father always told me: **Anything worth doing is worth doing right.**

WHAT THIS BOOK IS... AND WHAT IT IS NOT

I am not going to sugar-coat the realities of what's involved because **there is only one way to write a book, and that is to sit your butt in a chair and write.** All the tricks and shortcuts in the world won't mean anything if you are not willing to do the work.

There are many *(too many)* books that preach how to write a book in a week or how to publish a book without having to actually write it!

Yes, there actually are books available that promote the idea of "writing" a book without actually writing it. That would be like hiring someone to cook a meal for you then calling yourself a chef and telling everyone that you cooked it yourself. That's not the way it works. We will talk about those types of methods, and why you should avoid them, in just a moment, but first, I want to remind you that the focus of this guide is for nonfiction books.

Why nonfiction?

Because they are easier to write. Mostly because they are shorter than a novel and require less time.

Not to mention, there are certain things you need to know when it comes to writing fiction, such as character arcs, plots, subplots, show don't tell, and avoiding on-the-nose dialog to name but a few.

That being said, it's worth noting that a lot of the information you will learn in this guide can also be used for fiction, I just don't recommend that you start with a full-length novel because it really is a lot of work.

Novels are also a harder sell than nonfiction books because many fiction buyers often stick to their favorite authors. We will discuss that a little later on too.

I have seen and read many books on how to avoid writing by using everything from hiring ghostwriters to buying PLR books (Private Label Rights) and then signing your name to it as the author with little to no work on your part. That's not what this guide is about.

They sound like a great way to fast-track having your own book but here's the thing: you may be able to fool people into believing that you wrote a book, but deep down you will always know that you didn't actually write it; you just put your name on someone else's work and claimed credit for it, much like the example I gave about hiring someone to cook for you then calling yourself a chef.

Putting your name on someone else's work is not *writing* a book… not by a long shot… and that's not what you'll learn from me!

I've broken the writing process down to help you succeed as quickly as possible, but at the end of the day, YOU have to write YOUR book.

The sense of pride you will feel when you hold your book in your hands, whether it's a paperback or an ebook on your Kindle, is something I want you to experience. Trust me, you are going to love it, and that is not something you can feel when you secretly know that you only put your name on someone else's work.

I will show you tips and tricks to help you with everything from outlining and formatting to publishing your book as a paperback and an ebook, but they are all designed to help people <u>who want to write their own book.</u>

So, let's get started…

Author's Note:

The ghostwriting I was referring to is not when a public figure hires a ghostwriter. Those ghostwriters spend a great deal of time with the public figure listening to their stories and ideas, taking notes and quotes, and then they put into words what it is the public figure wants to say. In short, they work together on the book, and the ghostwriter does the physical writing part.

The ghostwriters I was referring to are the ones who offer to write your book with little to no input or effort on your part. You tell them what you want the book to be about and they write it for you. And because it is a work-for-hire agreement, you own the copyright to what they wrote, and you can legally put your name on it as the author even though you didn't write a single word.

Using PLR books is essentially the same thing, but instead of hiring a writer and telling them what you want your book to be about, you simply find a PLR book already written and then pay for the rights to publish it as your own.

These writers make their money by selling the rights to their work, but they don't sell exclusive rights. That means, someone else could publish a book that is almost identical to yours because that person also paid for the rights to publish the same PLR book.

Can you imagine how embarrassing it would be when it was brought to your attention that someone else wrote a book just like yours, but instead of being able to sue for copyright infringement, you have to admit to your family, friends and peers that you didn't actually write the book… you just put your name on it and took credit for it.

I would never want to be put in that embarrassing situation; I'm sure you don't either.

WHAT'S YOUR BOOK ABOUT?

Selecting a topic for your book has never been easier! People are hungry for information and they are looking to the Internet, and places like Amazon, to feed that hunger.

There are countless topics that could be turned into a marketable book; the hardest part is often just deciding which one you want to write first.

By the time you finish reading this guide, you will feel confident enough to choose the topic of your book, or you could use one of the ideas presented in this guide.

Don't worry about 'stealing' mine or anyone else's ideas. For starters, **ideas cannot be copyrighted**, and secondly, if we both wrote a book on the exact same topic, they would be two different books anyway because we each have our own experiences to draw from, and we each have our own writing style.

Finding a topic you are passionate about will make writing about that niche much easier, and you will have a book to position yourself as an authority figure, which will in turn help generate more sales for your business and for your book.

There are countless marketing websites and books that tell you to first find a subject that has a high likelihood of selling, and then write a book about that niche regardless of your interest level or even if you have any knowledge or experience.

I don't recommend that method for first-time writers because the likelihood of failing – failing to finish the book and failing to sell it if you do – is just too high.

As you get more comfortable writing and publishing, and if you want to turn book publishing into a profitable business, then yes, finding niches that sell well and then writing about it is a great way to earn money because you will know how to do the necessary legwork, such as researching the topic and interviewing experts in the field, so that your finished book will be worth buying.

Until that time, **it is best to start with topics you are passionate about**, or at least interested in it enough that if someone asked you for help, you would be happy to talk to them about that topic.

It's more difficult to write your first book than it is your tenth, so start with a topic you actually like, and your chances of finishing your book, and your chances of actually selling it, will be greatly increased.

Don't be another statistic of yet another wannabe writer who never completed their book because you started off by writing about something you thought had a better chance of selling rather than writing about something you are knowledgeable and passionate about.

Be the exception to the rule and finish your book.

FINDING BOOK-WORTHY TOPICS

If you have several hobbies and interests but you're not sure which one to write about first, think about what problems you have recently solved. Chances are, other people have the exact same problem and are looking for a solution. **Your book could be the answer they are looking for!**

Start by drawing a line down the middle of a sheet of lined paper. In the left column, write down your hobbies, interests, and the jobs you've had. List also every problem you personally solved over the years, whether it is being more productive at work, finding a better way to study or memorize dates to how to bake cookies without burning the bottoms, or how to save money on your water bill.

You'd be surprised at how much you really do know when you start brainstorming all the things you have actually accomplished.

Most people think 'accomplishments' must be something grand, like climbing Mount Everest, and as such, they feel they haven't really accomplished much in life, let alone accomplishing anything worth writing about. But the reality is, for many people, something as simple as learning how to copy all their contacts, messages, and photos from their old cellphone to their new cellphone feels like they just conquered Mount Everest!

As you create your list, don't worry about whether or not your ideas or the problems you've solved could be turned into a worthwhile book. For now, just write them all down in the left-hand column. Use as many sheets of paper as you need.

People love to read how others have solved a problem that they currently have, so brainstorm a list of problems in your life and in the lives of your family, friends, and peers that you've encountered and helped them solve.

Are people always coming to you for help about something? Fixing computers, setting up cellphones and tablets, how to make a flakier pie crust, how to do basic car maintenance, how to build a deck or shed, how to grow your own herbs or vegetables, or how you lost so much weight without starving yourself are just a few examples of things people are often looking for help solving.

Maybe your grocery bill was getting out of control and you figured out the best way to use coupons. 'Coupons' doesn't sound like a very exciting or profitable book, but maybe you were embarrassed about using coupons, which means your personal story about how you overcame that problem because you needed to save money is something that a lot of people are still going through.

A book that helps them face and solve the problem of being embarrassed to use money-saving coupons, that also contains tips and tricks on how to use coupons to buy in bulk to save money, and how to safely store and freeze certain items, is helping them solve a lot of problems.

Who wouldn't be willing to spend a few dollars to have multiple problems solved in a single book?

There are hundreds if not thousands of every day problems waiting for solutions that the average person wouldn't even consider writing a book about because it seemed too simple.

But here's the thing…

If you had that problem, you can bet that many other people have the exact same problem, and they are waiting for someone like you to come along to help them solve it.

When you finish your list, draw another line down the middle of the right-hand column to divide it into two more columns, for a total of three columns on your sheet.

In the middle column, give yourself a score of 1 to 10 on how passionate you are about each subject you listed in the first column (a score of 1 being little to no interest; and a 10 being extremely passionate about the subject.)

Hobbies and interests will obviously have a higher score than things you can do but do not particularly like. That being said, don't immediately dismiss those jobs or tasks you dislike because within that subject might be a subtopic you really do enjoy.

For example, before the days of cellphones and free nationwide calling, I worked for a company selling long distance plans. Their cold-calling scripts were not particularly good, or effective, so I studied a bunch of books and audio tapes on sales, telephone sales, and cold-calling techniques so I actually knew what I was doing. I then wrote my own phone scripts, which in turn increased my sales and the commissions I earned.

When the sales manager noticed how quickly I went from being constantly hung up on to becoming one of their top-selling agents, he asked for permission to let my coworkers to use my scripts so they could sound more natural and be more efficient on the phone… but I still hated cold calling, and I eventually left that job.

A couple of weeks later I received a phone call from the sales manager; he invited me to sit in on their meeting with the vendor of a new service they were going to be selling. The sales manager wanted me to write the cold-calling scripts for that new line of business rather than using the vendor-supplied scripts because he knew the ones I could write would be effective.

So even though I disliked the job of cold-calling people, I would still rank that subject fairly high because I was passionate about writing, and I had a knack for writing sales scripts that sounded natural, which means I could turn that topic into a book I would enjoy writing.

If I simply wrote "cold calling" as something I did as a job and left it at that, it would have received an exceptionally low rank because I really do loathe cold calling. So much so that when I later founded my own advertising company, I hired people to make cold calls just so I would not have to do it, but that's another story.

FINDING YOUR AHA MOMENT

As you write your list and start ranking them on a scale of 1 to 10 you might get one or more 'Aha' moments and discover a topic that you enjoy and really want to write a book about, but I urge you, don't stop.

Not yet.

Keep listing and ranking everything you can think of because you can, and should, use this list for your second, third, fourth and subsequent books.

When you exhausted everything you can think of, go back to the top of your list and go over it again and think of how those topics could be further broken down.

This is why it is called brainstorming… you have to think of, and list, every possible idea regardless of how silly it may seem at the time. Write it down… because buried somewhere in those jobs or tasks you dislike might actually be a subtopic you do enjoy!

You can put an asterisk next to your 'Aha' topics for now – just don't settle on it just yet... there's a bit more work that needs to be done before you start writing your book.

In the last column, you will rank your book ideas according to some research you are going to be doing a little later in this guide. I call it *"The Amazon Test."*

In short, the ideas that you ranked high as being passionate about you are going to search for those topics on Amazon to see if there are other books on that topic, and how well they sell.

Topics that rank low in sales you will give a lower score and topics that generate a lot of sales will rank higher. Best sellers will be ranked a 10. We will cover how to find the 'real' sales rank in more detail a little later on.

When you finish ranking the sales potential for the topics on your list, you will have a more focused idea of what topics would make a good book because you're not only passionate about the topic, you know it also has decent, if not great, sales potential!

Just remember that you will only be ranking the sales potential for topics that you scored high for passion rather than every item on your list, unless you just happen to enjoy research, which could be an idea for a potential book: helping others learn how to enjoy research.

With your list complete and the most passionate ideas ranked for their sales potential, all you need to do now is pick one and start outlining and writing your book, which we will cover in a future chapter.

Anything you marked with an asterisk for your 'Aha' moment that also ranked high for both passion and sales potential is probably what your first book should be about.

So Write it!

FINDING BOOK-WORTHY IDEAS

Google is your Friend

If you own a cellphone or a computer, you already have the most powerful tool you need to find a niche topic to write about. Go to Google and type *"How do I"* and see what Google autofills below your question.

Google's results will change over time, so you should search for topic ideas when you are ready to pick a new topic for your book rather than relying on the results of an old search because it most likely is a bit outdated.

When I was writing the first draft of this book, I went to Google and typed *"How do I"* and these are the results I received:

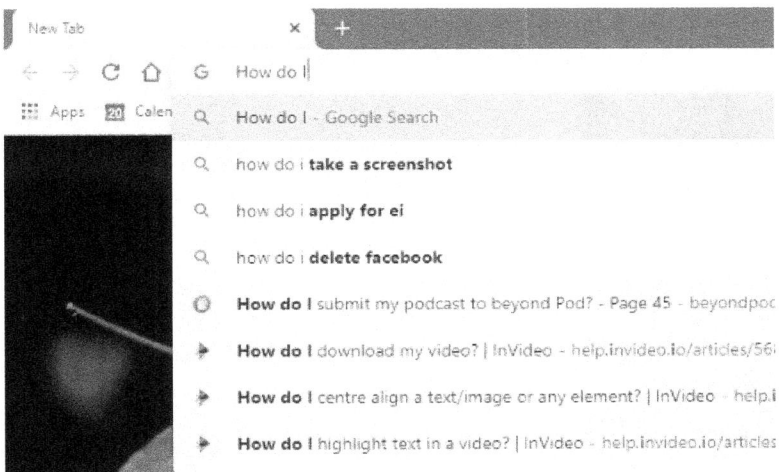

I then changed the question and asked, *"What's the best way to"* and received the following results:

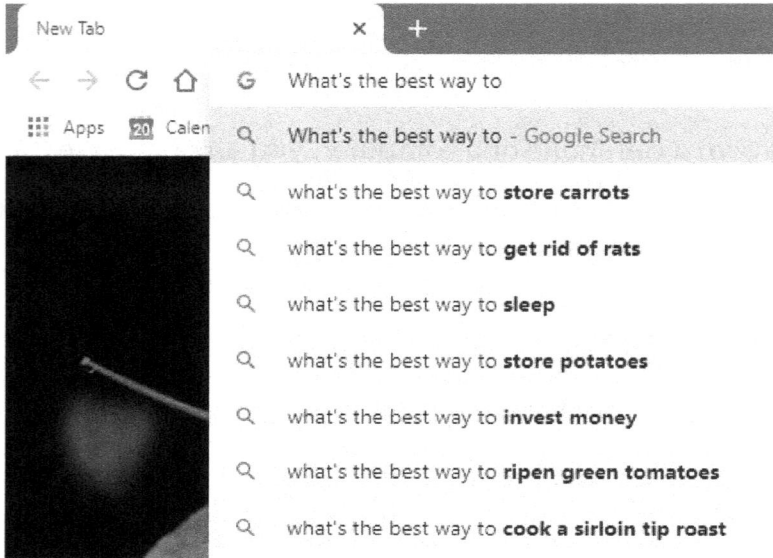

I then changed that question to simply *"Best way to"* to show you that simply rewording the question will give different results.

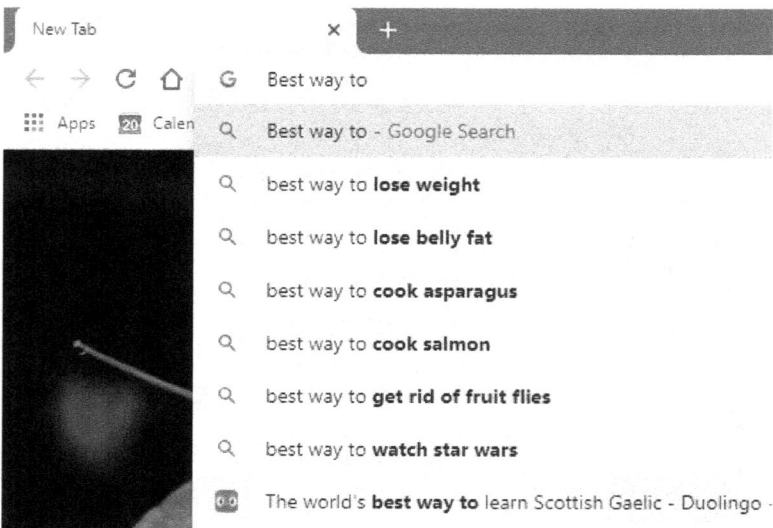

My results leaned heavily towards cooking because I do I lot of cooking and often search for various recipes. Google knows this because of the cookies (no pun intended) on my computer, so of course it will list my interests, but it also displays what other people are actively searching for on Google.

Author's Note:

According to these Google results, apparently a lot of people have problems with rats and fruit flies because Google warranted it showing up as a suggested search. If you have a solution, writing about how to deal with various types of pests and vermin could be a potential book idea if it passes 'The Amazon Test' (more on that shortly.)

Google may be your friend, but Amazon will become your new Best Friend because **the best place to search for profitable book topics is on Amazon itself.**

In the screenshot below, I changed the drop-down menu on Amazon's search bar from "All Departments" to "Books" and then typed my query.

I simply typed the word 'cook' to show you that you do not need questions or long phrases for Amazon to start autofilling what books people are actively searching for.

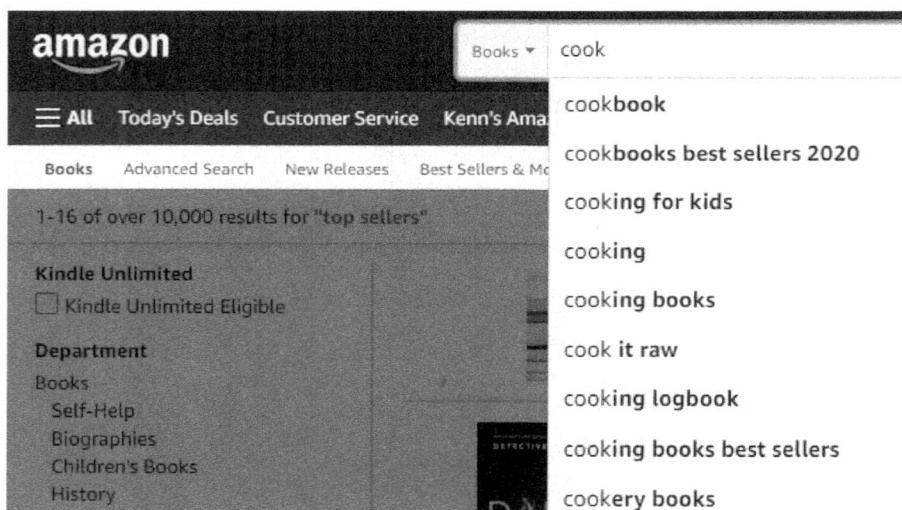

"Cookbook" was the first suggestion followed by *"cookbooks best sellers 2020", "cooking for kids"* and so on.

If your passion idea has to do with cooking but you weren't quite sure if you should write a cookbook with recipes or a 'how-to cook' guide, you can 'drill down' to see if there is a market for your idea by selecting one of the suggestions that Amazon autofilled.

When I clicked on *"cookbooks best sellers 2020"* it revealed the Top three best-sellers followed by several others.

In the next section we'll cover 'The Amazon Test' to help you decide if your book topic is worth writing about. This is especially important if you want to actually *sell* your book rather than just writing it for the sake of writing a book on that topic.

But, as previously mentioned, if you want to write a book on a certain topic you are passionate about and don't care about how many books to sell, then go ahead and write the book you always wanted to write.

THE AMAZON TEST

A common mistake that new writers often make is believing that if there are a lot of books in their niche already, writing another one is a bad idea because the market is over saturated. In reality, the opposite is true…

Not having any competition, or very little competition, is usually a sign that writing a book in that niche is probably a bad idea if your goal is to actually sell your book rather than just writing it.

Unless it is a brand-new product or service that just hit the market, it most likely means there is no competition in that niche because people are not interested in buying books on that particular topic.

When it comes to selling books, competition is a good thing!

The more books there are on a topic (and if they have sufficient sales) it means there is a lot of demand for that type of book.

Competition that have decent sales is a good thing because it tells you that people are not just searching online for information, **they are willing to spend money on a book to have their problem solved**.

That is something Google cannot do.

Google, as great as it is for finding information, only shows you what people are actively looking for (the problem they need answered) while **Amazon narrows your search to see if people are willing to pay for that answer.**

If you only wanted to write and grow a blog, then Google has plenty of information to help you find what people are searching for to help you decide if there is an audience for your blog. However, as the author of a book, an audience looking for free information is not enough; you want to make sure there is a market for your book, and that's where Amazon is your new best friend.

Not only can you find if there are books being sold, but you can also use the *'Look Inside'* feature of the top books to get a better idea of what those best-selling books look like – the formatting, fonts, and even the size (physical size and the page count) of those books.

If you want to write about a certain topic and really don't care if there's a market for it, then go ahead and write your book.

But…

If you want to do more than just share your ideas, in other words, you want to make money rather than just giving your experience and expertise away, then you should spend a bit of time researching your niche on Amazon to verify that there is a market for a book like the one you want to write.

We will cover that in the next section but first, let's look at a real-world example of why you should care about sales and your book's market potential.

Back in the day, one of my passions was performing as a ventriloquist. Even though I have since retired from performing and no longer do it, I still have all my puppets, and I always wanted to write a book on ventriloquism.

So why didn't I write it yet?

Some quick research within Amazon told me that ventriloquism is, sadly, a dying artform; most of the books being sold are from 15-20 years ago and they are not huge sellers.

Because my primary focus now is building my publishing business (translation: making money writing and selling books) it doesn't make sense for me to spend the time required to write, edit, send it to beta readers, design or hire a cover artist, then publishing a book on ventriloquism regardless of how passionate I am about the subject because the market for those books is just too small.

But Kenn, maybe people are just waiting for a new book to come along because, like you said, there are not a lot of books on the subject and most of them are fifteen to twenty years old?

That may be true, but right now it is a gamble as to whether there are enough people willing to purchase a new book on ventriloquism, and it is a gamble I do not wish to make.

Even though books can be self-published with no upfront costs, it still costs time… and because my primary focus right now is building my publishing business, my time would be better spent writing books that have a larger market and a higher potential of selling.

Keep in mind that my advice that your first book should be on topics you are passionate about rather than just sales potential is so that you, the first-time writer, do not get overwhelmed during the writing process and give up before you finish your book.

As you gain more experience and find your writing voice, you'll have a much better chance of finishing books that have a larger market even if you're not overly passionate about the subject.

Contrary to what some 'gurus' will tell you, first-time writers should not focus on finding profitable niches and then writing about them because, for the lack of a better way of putting it: People are not stupid.

It will not take them long to discover whether or not you actually care about the subject, and the last thing you want to be labeled is a fraud who's only in it for the money.

If you don't care about your book, nobody else will either.

The Amazon Test to find your book's marketing potential is to help you decide which book to write about from all the ideas you ranked high for passion, not just finding a profitable niche regardless of your interest level.

AMAZON'S BSR

Amazon's Best Sellers Rank (BSR), also known as the 'Amazon Sales Rank' is a score that Amazon assigns a specific product, such as books, based on sales data gathered over a period of time.

To get a better idea if books in a particular niche are selling, you simply need to look at their overall sales rank to determine if there is a demand for that type of book. The lower the number the better, but just because a book has a great BSR in one of the subcategories doesn't necessarily mean it's selling well.

Allow me to explain….

One of the 'hacks' some people discovered is that they can place their ebook in a less-than-popular subcategory and give their ebook away for free. Next, they get a few of their friends to 'purchase' the free ebook. Because it has several new 'purchases' all at the same time, the ebook jumps to the #1 spot in that vague subcategory. They then grab a screenshot of their ebook listed in that top spot, raise the price of their ebook, then add '#1 Best Selling Author' to their marketing materials to help generate sales when in reality, their "#1 Best Selling Book" never even made so much as a single penny in sales.

I read an article about an author name Brent Underwood who spent less than three dollars and five minutes of his time on Amazon publishing the ebook: *Putting My Foot Down: A Book Featuring My Foot,* and that's exactly what his ebook was: a blank book featuring a lone cover photo Underwood snapped of his foot. His plan (using a hack similar to the one I described) was borne out of frustration at the online publishing industry. He did it to show people how easy it was to have a 'Best Seller' even if the book is blank. Unfortunately, it was once an honor to have your indie published book deemed a best seller, but the title has since become almost meaningless.

The screenshot below shows a self-help ebook about how to be present in the moment is ranked as a #1 Best Seller in the 'Geology in Earth Sciences' subcategory. Obviously, that ebook has nothing to do with geology, but it does show why being a #1 Best Seller in one of Amazon's subcategories doesn't mean much anymore.

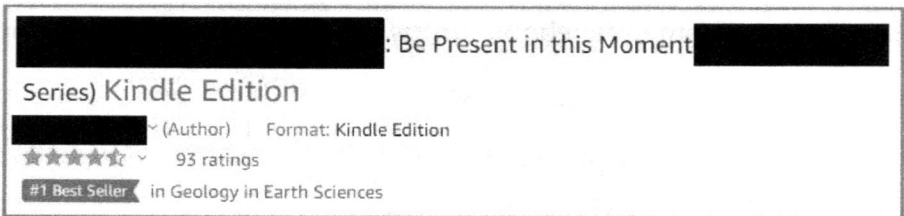

NOTE: *I blanked out the main title and the author's name because I do not wish to imply that they did it on purpose.*

When you upload your book to Amazon you select two categories for your book and Amazon picks a third category for you, and sometimes Amazon picks an incorrect category based on the title. If the book is placed in a not-very-popular category, and you start getting sales, it's naturally going to jump to the top spot because not a lot of books are typically sold in that less-than-popular category to begin with.

If your book is miscategorized, I wouldn't use that ranking in your marketing materials because savvy book buyers will quickly see it's not really a #1 Best Selling book.

The reason I am telling you this is so that you don't beat your head against a wall chasing a top rank in one of those subcategories just so you can add "Best Selling Author" to your marketing materials. It may look impressive to your family and friends, but it's widely known to indie book publishers and savvy buyers that it doesn't really mean much anymore.

That being said, if you do reach "Best Seller" status in a broader category that you book actually belongs in (through organic sales or paid ads) there is nothing wrong with mentioning it in your marketing materials to help you sell even more books because you've earned it.

And don't fret too much if your book doesn't get listed as a best seller in your subcategory because there's a good chance that it was, you just missed it because BSRs change constantly... you could have a #1 Best Seller or be listed in the top 10 but an hour later, be ranked #50.

Instead, focus on writing the best book you can and marketing the heck out of it to raise your BSR naturally, and have the book royalties to back it, rather than focusing your attention on being able to list yourself as a Best-Selling Author in a subcategory.

Remember that the BSR number is just an overview... books ranked at #100,000 or less <u>for ALL BOOKS</u> (not a subcategory) have decent to great daily sales, whereas a #1 book in one of the lesser-known subcategories could only be selling a book or two a month, sometimes less.

WHAT ASIN IS AND HOW IT CAN HELP

ASIN stands for Amazon Standard Identification Numbers, which are unique blocks of 10 letters and/or numbers that identify items. You can find the ASIN on any item's product information page on Amazon. For printed books, the ASIN is the same as the ISBN number, which stands for the International Standard Book Number, which is a unique number assigned to each book.

When you are self-publishing a printed book, the best action you can take is to get your own ISBN. Ebooks do not require an ISBN, which is often why many authors only publish ebooks instead of print versions, because they don't have to buy an ISBN.

I have my own publishing company and can assign ISBN numbers to my books; if you are not a book publisher, you have to either purchase an ISBN or use a free ISBN that Amazon will assign your book.

But Kenn, I heard that ISBNs can cost up to $100 or more, why would I pay for one if Amazon will assign my book one for free?

When potential buyers read your book's information it also tells them the name of the publisher. All printed books that have free ISBNs assigned to them by Amazon are listed as 'Independently Published.'

Having a book listed with a publishing company, even if it is your own publishing company, looks *'more professional'* than an indie-published book.

Unfortunately, buyers have discovered that 'Independently Published' books are sometimes not very good because there is no one doing any quality control other than the author, and those books are often released without the benefit of an editor or even beta readers.

Sadly, there are many independently published books that are riddled with typos, bad grammar, formatting issues and so on because the author doesn't have anyone to 'tell them' to put more time and effort into their book because it really does matter.

One of the reasons why I wrote this guide is to help you bring your book to the next level, so I would be remiss if I didn't tell you that having your own ISBN number can help differentiate your book from all those less-than-stellar books so it is not *'lumped in with them'* by also being listed as 'independently published.'

No, it's not fair... but the authors who publish shoddy books, either through ignorance or just not caring because they're trying to make a quick buck, are the reason why independently published authors are given a bad reputation, and they perpetuate the myth that self-published books are substandard to 'real' books.

However, if your book cover is professional looking, your description is well thought out, and the 'Look Inside' option doesn't reveal a bunch of typos and poor grammar, most people don't care if it is independently published. They buy nonfiction books because they have a problem to solve; if your book has the solution they are looking for, that's all that really matters to them.

If you only plan on writing one or two books as a hobby, then you may not see a benefit of spending money to purchase an ISBN, but if you plan on publishing books as a second source of income, or maybe someday becoming a fulltime writer, using Amazon's free ISBN numbers right away may not be the best option for you.

Like everything else when it comes to self-publishing, the choice is yours.

Let's get back to the Amazon Test...

For the Amazon Test you want to copy the book's ASIN (or ISBN) and use that in one of the online calculators to determine approximately how many sales per month that book is actually getting, rather than just going by the BSR which is constantly changing every day, sometimes hourly for more popular items.

Remember my ventriloquism book idea?

Pasting the ASIN (ISBN) numbers from other ventriloquism books into the various online tools is how I determined that ventriloquism books are typically not great sellers.

When a ventriloquist is on or wins contests like the 'X Factor' or one of the 'Got Talent' shows, or well-known ventriloquists like Jeff Dunham releases a special, the interest in ventriloquism suddenly goes up, and more books on the subject get sold. But then the sales drop again when that fleeting interest wanes because ventriloquism is a niche hobby; it's not one of the mainstream classic hobbies that always have an audience, and market, for new books.

Working with the various online tools to search for books to determine a niche's profitability is beyond the scope of this book, but a quick Google search for 'Amazon ASIN Calculator' will get you started to learn the ins and outs of determining a niche's potential.

Doing all that work is to help you decide which book idea from your passion topics list has the best chance of selling, but as previously mentioned, if you are only interested in writing about a topic you are passionate about and you are not concerned about making money selling your ebook, then by all means, write the book you always wanted to write.

However…

Before you convince yourself that just being able to help people is reward enough, I urge you to pay close attention to the next section.

WHY YOU SHOULD CHARGE FOR YOUR EBOOK

Until recently, I really didn't care about sales; I just wanted physical books so my kids and grandkids would have something to remember me after I am gone, so I gave the ebook versions away for free because I was not interested in making money from my writing.

But I discovered (the hard way) that most people place more value on things they actually paid for. People generally perceive things they pay for as being more valuable, and more worthy of their time, than something they got for free.

Yes, we all like getting free stuff, but how many free ebooks have you personally downloaded and never got around to reading yet?

I'm guilty of that too.

My Kindle has dozens of free ebooks on it that I downloaded years ago but never got around to reading yet, but the couple of dozen ebooks that I paid for just in the last year alone I have actually read.

If your primary goal really is to help people rather than making money, know that you'll be able to help a lot more people by charging them for your ebook than you will by giving it away for free.

Why?

Because when people pay something for your ebook, even if it is a modest 99 cents, **there's a much better chance that they'll actually read it than if they downloaded it for free**.

You can't help people if they don't read your book!

If you really want to help people, make them pay for your book!

CAN I WRITE A NOVEL INSTEAD OF NON-FICTION?

Absolutely.

Just keep in mind that nonfiction books are in high demand because the people searching Amazon are looking for ways to solve a problem, and **the people on Amazon are ready, willing and able to buy**… if they weren't, they'd be on Google wading through the countless pages of free information instead.

Topics such as improving their lives and making more money are always of interest to people. For these books, just about any author will do, even unknown writers, because they're looking for answers. **If you can solve their problem, then you are the author for them!**

However, most people searching for fiction are usually looking for a book by one of their favorite authors, and until you build a big enough reputation, chances are your fiction book won't be on their "Buy Now" list.

This is not meant to dissuade you from writing that novel you always wanted to write. If there's a story in you that you have to tell then by all means, tell it. I'm merely suggesting that before you jump in headfirst to see if you sink or swim as a novelist, it might be better to test the waters and find your writing voice with a shorter, nonfiction book instead.

Like everything else, that choice is yours... don't let me or anyone else tell you otherwise, especially if you dream of writing your opus.

However, if you're in it for the money, and there is nothing wrong with that, it's been frequently said that **the quickest route to book publishing profits is in the nonfiction ebook market.**

This is for a number of reasons:

- Fiction readers often like to curl up in a chair with an actual paperback novel. If you only have an ebook available, you limit your sales potential. People looking to solve a problem don't care about being able to curl up in a chair, they just want to solve their problem, and shorter, ebooks are often where they look for those answers.

- Fiction readers tend to purchase books and ebooks from authors they are already familiar with.

- To try and compete with more well-known authors, many fiction writers give their ebook away for free in hopes that the reader will purchase the sequels. This can be a good strategy *if* you already have those sequels completed, but if you're writing your first book, the only thing you will accomplish by giving it away for free is to introduce yourself to the world to try and build your name as an author. Actually making money at it will take a bit longer. More on this shortly. Just remember what I said earlier about the value people place on free stuff. If you want to build your reputation as an author, sell your ebook rather than giving it away.

- Fiction is more difficult to write and deliver well. Thinking of a great story is not the same as _writing_ that great story. Many first-time authors fail to deliver a great reading experience because they don't understand what it takes or how to write creatively without using boring cliches or worse, they use stale, unrealistic descriptions and dialog. Dialog is by far the hardest part to 'get right' when writing fiction.

- Many of the classics in fiction are now available as free ebooks. Convincing readers to purchase fiction from an unknown author is a tougher sell when so many books are available for free by authors trying to build their fanbase and sell the sequels, and by the countless classics that have fallen into the public domain because their copyright has expired.

- Public domain nonfiction books are outdated and often of no use to modern problems needing modern solutions, which is why there is always a demand for great, new nonfiction books.

IDEAS YOU CAN USE FOR NON-FICTION BOOKS

The one group of people who are always willing to buy nonfiction books are hobbyists. Their passion can be your financial gain because at any given time, **avid hobbyists are willing to spend money on their hobbies.** And the one thing hobbyists always want is more information on their hobby.

Notice I didn't say it is what they *need*, but rather, what they *want*?

Hobbyists always want more information, and one of the best ways to give them what they want is a book on their hobby.

Facebook and other sites have online groups dedicated to specific hobbies, making them a great place to learn what problems hobbyists currently have because that is where they talk and help each other out by sharing ideas, exchanging testimonials for products and services, and recommending useful books that they've read.

Enthusiasts come in all shapes and sizes and from all walks of life: golfers, hikers, gardeners, wine connoisseurs, video gamers, and people who collect vintage sports cards.

Some hobbies seem to continually attract enthusiasts, like playing golf, restoring old cars, watching football and other mainstream sports, as well as listening to music by their favorite artists. These are the 'classic' hobbies that never seem to fade while others seem to come and go because they are just a fad.

Do you remember country line dancing? Plenty of people still do it, but it's not nearly as popular as it once was. If you've never heard of it, that should give you an idea of how much a fad can fade… sometimes into obscurity.

If you get in early on a new fad you could sell quite a few books, just know that it doesn't have a lot of 'staying power' because when those fads fade, so will your book sales.

Sticking to the 'tried and true' hobbies will help you create a steadier stream of income for a longer period of time.

Evergreen content, which is content that is continually relevant for readers over a long period of time, has the greatest staying power. **Books with evergreen content create a steadier and longer-lasting stream of income because it's never outdated.**

It's worth noting, and I shouldn't have to say this but it's better to be safe than sorry, **you should actually be interested in the hobby in order to write a useful book on it.**

As already mentioned, some self-publishing "gurus" will preach the method of finding a need and filling it to sell books. Just remember that it's not their reputation that could be ruined by just finding and filling a need and then being 'called out' as a fraud because you don't actually know what you are talking about. Just filling a need, especially when it comes to hobbies, could prove to be disastrous.

You may be able to fool some of the people some of the time, but enthusiasts knowledgeable in their hobbies will quickly discover that you really don't know what you are talking about, or you're just rehashing old, outdated information you found online to sell a few books.

They'll also be quick to make sure their fellow enthusiasts know you're a fake.

With the right amount of dedicated research and interviewing the right people, you can write a useful book on a topic you initially knew nothing about (that's what research and interviews are for) but at the end of the day, the chances of you giving up before you finish your book because it's simply too much work is greatly increased because you're writing about a subject you don't actually care about.

It's just not worth the risk.

The best way to make sure you actually finish your hobby-themed book is to write about hobbies you care about, hence creating your list and scoring them from 1 to 10.

Use Facebook groups and Amazon searches to narrow down the topic of your book to make it useful and relevant, but I think it is best to stick to topics that interest you.

In time, when you get more experience writing and publishing books, you can 'stray off the path' to write other books.

For example, if you are a man, you might find it difficult to write a credible book that's helpful to brides-to-be, but as you gain more experience and learn how to properly research and interview people, there is no reason why you cannot write such a book... I just don't recommend that you start off too far outside the box.

Online Training

There is really no limit on the marketability of how-to books and courses. Just about everyone wants advice and encouragement so that they can do anything they read in a how-to book or learn from an online course; that's what those books and courses are for after all.

A great resource for finding book topics is to search the current best-selling courses on sites like Coursera, Udemy, Teachable and others.

I got started teaching online courses by turning one of my how-to books into an online course called *"Sell More Products without Facebook Ads or PPC Advertising."* I created a second course based off of one of my hobbies called: *"Learn The Fundamentals of Screenwriting & Story Structure"*, and I'm working on a third course. Who knows, maybe someday this book will become an online course as well.

If you're interested in creating an online course to supplement your book and build your brand as an authority figure, that too is something to consider, but let's not get ahead of ourselves, focus on writing that amazing book first!

The possibilities, and the potential to earn money, are endless.

Non-fiction books don't just have to be about hobbies. Life itself often requires instruction. Here are just a few examples of ideas that can be turned into instructional books:

- How to write a screenplay
- How to sell used items online
- How to have a successful garage sale
- How to organize your home office
- How to shoot a short film on your cellphone
- How to talk to teens so they'll listen
- How to deal with Crohn's (or some other illness)
- How to cook on a budget
- How to use a slow cooker with recipes (or smoker, or how-to BBQ to name just a few)

The How-To Book Title

The book titles I suggested all start with the words 'How to.' This is because it simplifies it for prospective buyers because the rest of the title tells them exactly what they will learn.

Consider these two titles for a book on how to have a garage sale:

1. "How to have a successful garage sale."

2. "One weekend away from a clutter free home"

Although the second title is clever, a little punchier, and does correspond with the book content, some people may confuse it for a book about how to organize their home as opposed to selling your unused items in a garage sale to get rid of the clutter.

If someone bought your garage sale book thinking it was about organizing their home, you can expect to get poor reviews because your book wasn't what they were actually looking for, and they'll feel as if you 'tricked them' into buying it with a confusing title.

The first title is not as punchy or exciting as the second title, but it sums up exactly what the reader can expect to learn from that book. Just remember that your subtitle is where you can get creative, like this:

How To Have a Successful Garage Sale:
One Weekend Away from a Clutter-Free Home.

Little Things Mean Big Things to Other People

Any part of life, from coping with life to the smallest things some people take for granted, can be the subject of a how-to book because _it is_ a big deal to other people.

For example, selling used items on Buy & Sell websites didn't look like that big of a deal because it seems pretty straight forward: List your item and how much you wanted for it.

The problem was, I found myself wasting a lot of time and energy trying to find items I wanted because the sellers had really crappy-looking ads, or their ad didn't give enough information. And it often took them forever to get back to me to answer my questions, if they got back to me at all! It was very frustrating. I was ready, willing and able to buy; too bad they weren't ready to actually sell.

I noticed a common theme across these less-than-desirable ads so in 2012, I decided to help them sell their items by writing a how-to ebook that I gave away as a free PDF. I wasn't interested in making money off the ebook, I just wanted to help other people make money by sharing what I knew from my days of owning and running an advertising company.

Remember what I said about the perceived value of free stuff?

It only received a handful of downloads so I wasn't really helping anyone, and I didn't know if they actually read it, so in 2015, I turned that little how-to PDF into an online course. But because I wasn't smart enough to learn from my mistakes, I also gave the course away for free to try and build my reputation as a course instructor.

A lot of students enrolled in my course, but my course's dashboard showed me that the vast majority of the students who enrolled never even started the course; they just enrolled because it was free, which meant I still wasn't actually helping people.

I then started charging for my course and it not only sold, nearly every student who paid for the course completed it. Now I was actually helping people (and making a bit of money doing it.)

How to make better ads to sell used items online didn't seem like that big of a deal to me, but according to my sales reports, and the raving reviews my students left when they completed the course, **it *was* a big deal to them**. So much so that one of my future projects is updating that little how-to guide I originally wrote back in 2012 so I can sell it on Amazon as a book and ebook… *IF* it passes *The Amazon Test*.

Looking Younger/Feeling Better

Teenagers want to look older, but from that point on, for most of the population in Western society, looking younger seems to be a common desire for men and women alike. Some people spend a great deal of money looking for the 'Fountain of Youth' whether it's in a bottle, by means of a special diet, through surgery, hair transplants, makeup, skin treatments, or found in the pages of a book. Beauty magazines fly off supermarket shelves for exactly that reason.

A book about staying young, looking younger, feeling healthier and losing weight will always have a solid future because of that desire. Here are just a few title ideas for potential books. I'm sure you can think of many more.

- Drop 10 Pounds in 10 Days
- Look 10 Years Younger
- 50 Ways to Look & Feel Younger
- How to Lose Weight Without Being Hungry
- Look & Feel Younger and Healthier
- Top 10 Ways to Lose Weight.

Botox, chemical peels, diets, vitamins, herbal teas and remedies, cellulite creams, hair dyes, gastric bypasses and the likes are being purchased all the time by middle-aged housewives, the elderly, and even women in their twenties because it seems no one wants to look their age these days, making these types of books a hot seller! It's also becoming more and more common for men to seek out these options as well.

Health

People without any medical credentials write and publish books on health all the time. Just make sure your book comes with a disclaimer that you're not a medical professional (unless you are) and that your readers should always seek professional, medical advice and speak to their family doctor before starting any diet, exercise program or treatment.

Money

Money makes the world go around, and so it would make sense that books on the topic of making money are in high demand.

Just like there is a never-ending stream of new diet books, there's always room for new books on the topic of making money. From getting rich to saving and investing, people are always interested in books on how to become wealthy and living the lifestyle they have always dreamed about.

I do not approve of or recommend writing any type of "Get Rich Quick" book because those schemes rarely, if ever, work, and you'll only hurt your own reputation and be labelled a scam artist.

Some of the people who publish those types of books make money by selling the promise found within the pages of their books, not by actually doing what they claim will make you rich. Don't believe the hype some authors throw at you about creating a six-figure income.

Think about it…

If you figured out a system that guaranteed you six figures a month, would you sell your secret for a mere $2.99 and create more competition for yourself so you're no longer making that six-figure income?

Of course not, that would be silly.

Most of those 'systems' are untested and were created for one reason - to sell their book to you!

That's why all those books come with a disclaimer that they don't make any promises or guarantees on how much money you make and that the results they share from all their case studies and accolades are not typical results and that your results will vary.

Yes, some people do make six figures and more, but they are the exception to the rule.

Seriously, if you were making six figures a month, would you put in the time and effort to write and publish a book, and then spend a small fortune promoting it just so you could sell it for a few dollars? Or would you be kicking back on a beach somewhere enjoying the good life?

Chances are, doing all that work to write and sell an ebook for a few measly dollars would be the last thing on your mind!

Many of those authors make their money by selling the promise, not by doing anything they say to do in their book, or they often have a huge following with a profitable mailing list, so anything they publish already has a built-in audience that are ready, willing and able to buy from them.

Their system may work for them, but there's a good chance it won't work for you because you don't have that built-in audience or the money and resources to advertise your book enough to generate those six-figure sales.

I'm not trying to lump every author with a 'make money' book into the same pile. Many of them have great books with proven systems, I'm merely suggesting that you do your due diligence so that you don't fall for the hype of those false promises, and I urge you to never become one of those "Get Rich Quick" authors who take people for a ride by publishing shoddy books with unproven tactics.

Life Enrichment

Self-help books are leaping off shelves at brick-and-mortar bookstores and from online retailers because people want the power to change and improve their lives.

People are always looking for ways to find peace with their past, how to find harmony or be spiritual in a consuming society, and how to find love.

There is no end to the how-to books you could create in the category of self-help or life enrichment.

Using the Latest Technology

We live in a society obsessed with having the latest and greatest technology.

Books on buying, using, and useful hacks to improve computers, cellphones, tablets, digital TVs, cameras, as well as software tips & tricks to the latest games and gaming consoles are other niches that seem to do well.

Home Improvement

Walk into any Home Depot or Lowe's and you will quickly discover that home improvement is a popular topic.

Most apartment dwellers and young students may not be in this particular niche market, but homeowners are, and they're always looking for ways to repair or improve their home.

There are entire cable channels dedicated to home improvement, so that should tell you that it is a big market with plenty of potential, especially in the DIY *(Do It Yourself)* niche.

Food

Another popular topic that also has plenty of shows on cable TV is cooking. Everything from recipes and cooking techniques to regional food and how to recreate favorite restaurant dishes make a large market and can be quite profitable.

On the topic of cookbooks:

If you decide to write a cookbook, I urge you to not be like some of the cookbooks I made the mistake of downloading...

As a former restaurant owner and someone who enjoys cooking and trying new recipes, the one thing that irked me about those poorly designed cookbooks was the lack of pictures.

It's been my experience that people looking to try new recipes want to know what the finished dish is supposed to look like. When the book doesn't have any pictures, they don't know. It's very frustrating.

If you're interested in writing a cookbook, there's an excellent chance that you own several cookbooks already. Flip through your favorites and chances are you will see plenty of pictures.

So why would people publish a cookbook without pictures when images are so important?

There are two reasons actually...

First, food photography is a skill. There is more to taking great-looking pictures of food than just pointing a camera at it and snapping the picture. As a photographer, and a former restaurant owner and cook who occasionally shares photos of the dishes I prepared, I can promise you that the lighting, the angle, the plate being used, the colors, and additional props all go into taking great pictures of food. It's not just a matter of point and shoot.

Secondly, including pictures for each recipe means the writer has to actually cook every dish in order to take those pictures. That can get quite expensive, and it drastically slows down the time it takes to publish the cookbook because no one wants to cook and throw-away all that food, so they most likely would want to cook the meal and then eat it after the pictures were taken.

This means a book with 150 recipes would take months to complete, even if they prepared one dish every day!

The authors of these less-than-stellar cookbooks that do not contain pictures either do not have the patience to wait that long, or they are just "collecting recipes" and then publishing them as a book.

I know of one self-proclaimed "Chef" who admitted that not only did he not have any formal culinary training (making him a cook, not a chef) but that he has more than 10,000 recipes that he collected over the years that he was releasing in a series of cookbooks.

Do you honestly think that he tested all ten thousand of those recipes to make sure the measurements and cooking times were accurate?

I've seen too many low-end cookbooks like this… the person who published the book was just copy and pasting recipes they found online and then published them as a cookbook.

The problem is, you have no way of knowing that the recipe wasn't accurate until after you wasted your money making it and had to throw it in the garbage because it wasn't edible.

If you want to write a cookbook, make sure they are recipes you have personally made so your readers are not throwing their hard-earned money away… and include pictures so people at least have an idea of what the finished dish is supposed to look like.

How-to Manuals for New Products or Services

Every new product or service that hits the market brings with it a need to be filled for the owners or subscribers to that product or service.

Targeting people who want to buy the most currently available item so they can learn how to get the most from that product or service should generate sales.

Anything To Do with Pets

People love their fur-babies, and they are pampering their pets more than ever. I know some people who treat their pets better than they treat other people, and those pet owners eagerly spend a small fortune on their pets.

Everything from homemade meals for picky eaters to training your pet, or even how to train your spouse to be more pet-friendly, will most likely fly off the virtual shelves because pet lovers are willing to pay good money for a book that helps them treat their fur-babies even more royally than they already do.

Part 2 – The Art and Act of Writing

The key thing to remember about writing, aside from the fact that you must sit yourself down and do the work, is not to overthink your book and stack it with too much information in an attempt to make it more 'worthwhile'.

Yes, giving people plenty of information is often appreciated, but too much information can also work against you. Many people look for shorter reads that they can consume quickly; most do not want to read a 350-page ebook that covers every possible scenario because **they are looking for a solution to their problem, not the answer to every possible question they could ever have**.

Yes, there is a market for those types of books, but most people live busy lives and prefer shorter reads, especially when it's in ebook form.

The average nonfiction book seems to be somewhere between 150 to 230 ebook pages. You can publish and sell books that are only 50 to 100 pages as long as the content is solid. It's better to have solid, clear information than to be rambling on just to make a higher page count. If it's less pages then a typical ebook then it's less pages; don't 'pad' your book with filler and fluff - it will slow the reading which may result and bad reviews, which in turn means less sales.

If your book has a print version, Amazon will use that page count for your ebook.

I've personally purchased a non-fiction ebook that was only 20 pages long and felt it was more than worth the money I spent; I've also purchased 300-page ebooks for less money that I never finished reading because it was cluttered with erroneous information, which created a boring read.

When you're writing your book, say what it is needed to make your point and then move on to the next section.

ON WRITING AND WRITER'S BLOCK

So what exactly is this dreaded "Writer's Block" that everyone is so scared of?

> **Writer's Block**
> /rīdərz 'bläk/
> phrase of writer
> the condition of being unable to think of what to write or how to proceed with writing.
> *"the novelist recovered from a two-year bout with writer's block"*

Even now, when I read that definition that I found online using a quick Google search, I still believe that some people use "writer's block" as a one-size-fits-all excuse rather than admitting to themselves, or to others, that the only reason they are not writing is because they are not writing. That's not just a play on words... most people who claim to be suffering from writer's block are using it as an excuse to make up for a poor work ethic.

But Kenn, don't you think that's a bit harsh? Just because you've never had writer's block doesn't mean it's not a real thing.

Sorry, but sometimes the truth hurts.

Writer's Block is a Myth. Some people claim to have writer's block as if they contracted a disease, but here's the thing… it doesn't exist. What they are experiencing is the self-inflicted phenomenon by writers who make choices that frequently, and inevitably, lead to failure.

You cannot write if you do not sit down and write; that's not some kind of 'block', it's simply the choice you made to not write.

Staring out the window instead of putting pen to paper, or typing on your computer, is a choice. Checking your email, Facebook and your other social media accounts, and the countless other activities people do, including those minor household chores you kept putting off but suddenly need to do, _instead of writing,_ are nothing more than choices. **The only thing you are really putting off is writing**.

Waiting for the elusive 'inspiration' to strike is not writing, it is the choice to not write. Waiting for that perfect opening to come to you, waiting to think of the best chapter heading before you write that chapter and so on are nothing more than excuses people use to try and explain why they are not writing. **There's only one way to write, and that's to sit your ass in a chair and write.**

There is no magic formula, there's no hidden secret, there is no such thing as writer's block... **you either make the choice to write, or you make the choice to not write.** As simple as it sounds, the only way to defeat the self-inflicted problem that some call 'writer's block' is to write your way through it.

If you get stuck, write something, anything, just keep writing. Write something silly, write something stupid, but keep writing!

The delete key is a wonderful thing. If you're not sure how to write something, *'talk your way through it'* by writing about why you are having trouble writing that section. As long as you stay in the habit of physically putting words to paper, the right phrase, or name, or whatever it is you are stuck on, will come to you. You can always go back and delete gibberish, but the minute you stop writing, you succumb to the self-inflicted myth called writer's block.

On Writing

The following excerpt is from a newspaper column I wrote back in 2002 that I believe sums up writing rather nicely:

Think of writing like a baby crawling around on the floor. One day, for no apparent reason, he simply decides to walk. He doesn't know why, it's just something he has to do. Something from deep inside makes him take that crucial first step and Wham! He falls flat on his diaper! Does the baby say, "I quit, I can't do this"?

No. Babies haven't yet learned the adult traits of self-doubt and fearing the unknown, he simply gets up and tries again.

The baby doesn't have high expectations of jogging down the street in his little Nikes and sweat suit after a few short attempts. Instead, he just takes it one wobbly step at a time.

The following day he continues to walk and fall, fall and walk, until one day the baby is walking as if he was born to walk. If only life could be so simple.

Well, it is. Sometimes you just have to look at it less like an adult and more like a child. You have a desire within you to write, but the self-doubting adult in you fears the unknown and stops you before you even try.

The adult in you is too embarrassed you might fall on your 'diaper', so you push writing, and most of your other desires aside as if they were nothing more than childish dreams.

Phooey on you! Let the child in you come out to play. Write something, anything, and satisfy that hunger within you.

Maybe what you write today won't be that good, but it doesn't matter, tomorrow it will be better. And better still the day after that until one day you'll be writing as if you were born to write.

If you have that little thing in you called "desire" then you have everything!

You were born to write, so write!

DON'T BORE YOUR READERS

If your book is nothing but stats and figures and step-by-step processes, even if that information is helpful or needed to get your point across, your readers will grow bored <u>if that's all you have to offer</u>, which will in turn result in poor reviews and low ratings, which means less sales.

So how do you get that needed information across without boring your readers to tears?

Through stories.

From the dawn of time, people have entertained and educated their children and each other through the use of stories. As previously mentioned, people enjoy reading how others have solved the problem they currently have, but they don't just want to read how you did it, **they want to know how it made you feel, and how your life was changed in some small, or big, way.**

In short, when they read personal stories of how a solution benefited you, they will be more inspired to try it for themselves.

When your readers are inspired by your personal stories, you will receive higher ratings and better reviews, which means more sales.

PAPERBACK OR EBOOK?

Personally, I like being able to hold a physical book in my hands, especially if it's a novel, and I know there are a lot of people who prefer paperbacks to ebooks.

I also know that there are many people who prefer ebooks regardless if it is fiction or nonfiction, because ebooks are usually less expensive, and often easier to read because they can adjust the fonts and font sizes on their Kindle, tablet, or whatever ereader or ebook software they use on their laptop or computer.

Kindle also includes *Whispersync,* which basically means if you switch devices, or "read" some of the book as an audiobook, it always updates to the exact spot where you left off, so you don't have to try and find the last page you read every time you switch devices.

Sometimes, I have 'Alexa' read the book to me on my Echo Dot. Amazon's Echo Dot is a smaller version of the original Amazon Echo smart speaker, and it looks more like a hockey puck than the Echo's original cylindrical shape.

Obviously, having Alexa read it is not going to sound nearly as good as an actual audiobook that you can purchase from Audible, but sometimes just being able to sit back and listen is preferred to physically reading the book yourself.

Author's Note:

At the time of this writing, I do not have my books available in the Audible bookstore, but that will change to give my readers yet another option to purchase my books, which in turn creates another income stream for me. Just know that recording an audiobook is very time consuming to do well.

For example, the full-cast audiobook version of my debut novel, Dead Hunt, took hours to edit each fifteen to twenty-minute episode, and I am an experienced audio engineer. If you are considering releasing your book as an audiobook, and if you do not have the necessary equipment or knowledge on how to narrate, record and edit audio, I recommend hiring a voice-over artist instead.

Not only do professional voiceover artists sound great, but they also give you completed audio files that will pass Audible's quality control specifications.

Just like editing and cover design, you can do it yourself, but sometimes it's easier, and you'll get much better results, by just hiring a professional in the first place.

But let's not get ahead of ourselves, focus on writing a great book first! I only mentioned audiobooks so you know that there is more than one way to deliver your book's content to consumers.

Let's get back to Paperbacks vs. Ebooks...

An added bonus to ebooks is Kindle devices have the X-Ray function which can give readers additional information, and Kindle devices can also be used to look up words with the built-in dictionary if needed.

Yet despite the many advantages of using an e-reader like the Kindle Paperwhite (the device I own) or a Kindle Oasis, some people still prefer a paperback version because there is something to be said about the feel and smell of the pages when you curl up with a good book, especially if it is a novel.

Armed with the knowledge that how people like to consume books is a personal choice, it makes more sense to me to create both a paperback and an ebook version, so my readers always have the choice of buying my books in the format they prefer. And I will be adding audiobooks in the future to give them another option if they'd rather listen than read.

One of the most important things you can remember when you're writing is that you are not typing a Facebook post, which are typically long, run-on paragraphs with horrible grammar, misspelled words, and they are often littered with short codes (acronyms) instead of using real words.

These types of posts (and books) are very difficult to read, so do yourself and your readers a favor and break those long paragraphs into shorter paragraphs.

Use a tool like Grammarly, which we will cover in another section, then relentlessly edit your manuscript. Then, when you think your book is perfect, send it to beta readers (we'll discuss them in a future section too) so they can help you make your book even better!

Most nonfiction books these days are released as ebooks because they are often cheaper to purchase, and because the buyer can have hundreds of ebooks on their Kindle at any given time.

I use my Kindle almost every day because, like most writers, I'm also an avid reader. But as I mentioned, when it comes to novels, I prefer a physical book.

I recently purchased the paperback version of a book by a screenwriter I met online. I quickly discovered that the gutters in his book were reversed - the right gutter was on the left and the left gutter was on the right, which meant each line was spaced too close to the spine where the pages were glued together, making it a bit difficult to read. Because I knew the author, I messaged him and let him know about that little glitch in the hopes that he would correct it to make it easier for other people to read his book.

Because I knew the author from an online group where he often posted a plethora of helpful advice, I knew his book would have a lot of useful information, and I most likely would refer to his book time and time again. This meant I would be constantly bending the pages back farther than normal just to read the words that were too close to the spine, causing excessive wear and tear; possibly causing the pages to fall out.

Not wanting to damage his book, I placed it on my bookshelf as a keepsake and ordered an ebook copy for my Kindle so I could actually read it.

I rarely buy two different versions of the same book. However, if I read an ebook that I thoroughly enjoyed, I sometimes go back and purchase a paperback version as a keepsake. If I am speaking to a friend or colleague whom I think would benefit from the book, I can quickly pull it from my bookshelf and give it to him or her as a gift, then repurchase another copy for my bookshelf.

OUTLINE YOUR BOOK

People who buy nonfiction books and ebooks are looking for solutions to a problem or more information on their hobbies, not necessarily entertainment, although adding personal stories is always recommended. They want nonfiction books to be informative, not filled with useless fluff. One of the best ways to do this is to brainstorm your idea first and write an outline rather than jumping in and just start writing.

There is no right or wrong way to outline your book; if it works for you, then it is the right way.

I suggest you first "mind map" (aka brainstorm) your book idea by using either index cards or mind mapping software. A quick Google search will give you plenty of results for free and paid mind mapping software, but index cards work just as well.

I've used index cards for outlining both fiction and nonfiction books. I have even used index cards to help me outline and organize online courses and the in-person workshops that I teach.

The idea is to think about all the main points you want to discuss in your book, and don't forget to include the things you wish you knew and what questions you had when you first started learning about that topic.

Google searches and Facebook groups dedicated to that topic are a great resource to discover what questions people are asking and what problems they are currently trying to overcome.

It's important to remember that the more experience we have and the more knowledgeable we become on a subject, the more we tend to forget what it was like when we first started learning about it. What is 'common sense' to us now wasn't so obvious when we were beginners, so don't assume your readers will know the basics unless you're writing a more advanced book on the subject for intermediate or advanced users rather than a book geared towards beginners or 'newbies'.

Write the main points you think people should know as a chapter heading on their own index card, and below that heading list three to five bullet points that should be covered on that topic.

Don't overthink what those chapter headings should be called. You can always go back and think of cool-sounding chapter titles when you're working on future drafts, for now, you just want a few words to describe what the main point is that you want to include in your book.

If one or more of those bullet points can be further broken down into several more subtopics, it might be better to move that bullet point to its own index card. I often write the topic headings in pen and the bullet points in pencil so I can erase them if needed and move a bullet point to its own index card as a new chapter heading.

Continue doing this until you have all the topic and subtopic ideas written down on index cards.

Chances are, by the time you finish brainstorming everything that you think is important, you may suddenly get overwhelmed and start believing that your book idea is just too big and will be too much work.

Don't panic!

This is where those index cards really help!

A CASE FOR OUTLINING AND USING INDEX CARDS

I discovered, the hard way, that it's a lot better to first outline the main ideas and subtopics on index cards so that I can decide what should and shouldn't be included in the book rather than putting in weeks or months of writing and then giving up because the project simply got too big and out of control.

When I first started writing how-to books, I made the mistake of jumping directly into writing without first outlining the book, and most of them are still collecting virtual dust on a hard drive somewhere because I got overwhelmed by the sheer size of it. Not to mention, I had only covered some the information I wanted to write about, and it was already too big. I eventually just gave up on that book idea and moved onto other projects. But… until I started outlining my books, most of those 'other projects' were never finished either.

Now I outline them… and I actually finish them!

LESS IS MORE

Brainstorming, by definition, means we are thinking of *every possible idea that 'could' be used*, but just because you wrote the topic or subtopic on an index card during a brainstorming session doesn't mean you have to actually use it!

When writers work on their second, third and subsequent rewrites, most of them discover that a lot of the information they wrote in their first draft is not really needed for several reasons, one of which is that **most beginners do not need that much information or they will be overwhelmed**.

So rather than doing all that writing only to delete it during a rewrite, index cards allow you to brainstorm all the topics and subtopics you can think of without having to physically write them all out.

So do not worry about how many index cards you used during your brainstorming sessions, because some of those topics can, and should be, omitted if the book would be better off without that additional, often superfluous, information.

One of the best things about first brainstorming your ideas to index cards or mind mapping software before you start writing, aside from the fact that it saves you a lot of time thinking about and typing countless pages that may eventually be deleted, is that you don't have to do it in chronological order… you can just fill out new index cards as ideas come to you regardless of where they will appear in your book.

Once you have all your index cards filled out, and if you have a large enough blank wall, a great way to organize your book is to use some of that blue 'sticky tack' and affix your cards on the wall. When you stand back and look at all your cards, you will start to see your book take shape.

You can easily move chapter headings (index cards) around until they are in the order that best gets your information across to the reader. Mind Mapping software is great for this because you can drag-and-drop to easily move things around, and you don't need a large blank wall, but sometimes just having a physical card to work with is more pleasing; it all depends on how "old school" you are and what you prefer.

I think mind mapping software is great and have used it on a few projects, but I often found myself 'fiddling' with the software too much by changing the fonts and colors for different topics, subtopics and so on rather than just brainstorming ideas.

The whole point of using mind mapping software in the first place was too brainstorm ideas, but that wasn't what I was doing, so using index cards instead was a better fit for me because it allowed me to focus more on the task at hand. Try them both and use whatever method works best for you.

Author's Note:

I originally used Post-it notes to brainstorm ideas, but sometimes I would go into my office to write and some of those Post-it notes were on the floor instead of on the wall where I put them. This is especially true if you use cheaper, off-brand sticky notes because the glue dries out that much quicker, or there is a window open and a gust of wind blew the sticky notes all over the room.

Not to mention, they often curled up, making them more difficult to read when I was standing back to get an overview of my book's outline. After that, I started using index cards and sticky tack because it was a better adhesive that didn't damage the wall, and my index cards didn't end up on the floor.

If you think there is too much information and some cards should be removed, I suggest that you don't actually remove the card from the wall. Instead, use a pencil to draw an X in the corner, or just flip the card over or upside down in case you need to come back to it later.

Once you have your book organized on the wall the way you like it, it's time to start writing your book.

You do this by simply taking down the first card, affix it to your computer monitor (or somewhere you can easily see it) and then write that chapter heading into Microsoft Word, Google Docs, Apple Pages, OpenOffice (or whatever word processing program you use) and then write about that topic and relevant subtopics that you listed as bullet points.

When you're finished writing everything you wanted to say about that topic, place a checkmark on the index card and affix it back on the wall. Then rinse and repeat for the next index card until you have everything written out.

If the book is shorter than you wanted, you can always go back to those crossed-out index cards and insert that topic and relevant subtopics into your written document. But chances are, once you finished elaborating on the topic and subtopics of each index card, you'll have to edit your book down rather than add to it.

Either away, just having those extra cards available means you don't have to "think" of what else you could include in your book... you already know what additional information can be added, and where, because all the cards from your brainstorming session are still on the wall in chronological order.

If you don't have a large enough wall to spread out your index cards, or you have small children who might move them around on you, it might be better to search for and use mind mapping software instead of physical index cards.

There's no right or wrong way, just the way that works best for you.

JARGON

Including too much technical jargon is never a good idea. The people reading how-to type books are looking for answers to a problem… **they have to be able to understand the answer, so keep it simple.** Any time you have to use jargon, make a point of explaining what that word or acronym means.

For example, if in your book you used the term ROI, some people, especially beginners (who are typically the ones buying introductory type how-to books) might not know exactly what ROI means. In that case you would type something like this:

ROI (Return on Investment)

…and then continue on from there.

Defining what acronyms and technical jargon means inside a set of brackets will be appreciated by your readers.

SLANG

It's always best to limit the amount of slang and local colloquialisms unless you are certain it is widely understood what those slang words or expressions mean.

For example, I live on an island on the East coast of Canada, but the majority of people who purchase my books are based in the United States, followed by the United Kingdom and Australia. If I used local slang that some of my fellow Cape Bretoners use it would confuse my readers. Here are just a few Cape Breton expressions:

- "Biff" – When you throw something
- "Conniption fit" – Really upset, really angry
- "Puck in the mout" – Punch in the face
- "Shootin' the drag" – Driving up and down the main street
- "Out runnin' the roads" - Out late at night or out all night
- "Givus a shot up da road" – Can you give me a drive?
- "Take a shot down later" – Come by later today

If I included some of those phrases in a story without explaining what they meant, the vast majority of my readers would have no idea what I was saying.

Discovering who your audience is comes with time and research. As I mentioned, I have been writing and publishing books and how-to courses since 2010. My sales reports tell me where those sales are coming from, so I know who my audience is from that and from my research into discovering what topic to write about next.

Most countries, other than the U.S., use the metric system. Because the majority of my readers are American, I use their measuring system (such as saying 6 x 9 inches instead of 15.24 x 22.86 centimeters) and I often use U.S. spelling (centimeter vs. centimetre) for the same reason.

It's a personal choice based on who buys the majority of my books; how you wish to present your book is entirely up to you.

EDITORS

Hiring an editor is also recommended but not required. When it comes to self-publishing there are no requirements per se, but that doesn't mean you should exclude certain things, like an editor.

We all make mistakes; typos are even found in professionally edited books by best-selling authors, so having a few typos here and there is not the end of the world. It's when your book is littered with mistakes that people lose interest and faith in you as a writer.

You *can* write and publish a book at no cost by doing it entirely by yourself, but using beta readers, an editor, and cover designer will make your book even better.

GRAMMARLY AND TTS (TEXT TO SPEECH)

Grammarly is a popular, free program that can help you find and correct most of the more common mistakes.

The method I use is slightly different and it is one I often recommend (and yes, I use Grammarly too) and that is to have your computer read it to you.

If you are using Microsoft Word, there is an option under the 'Review' tab called 'Read Aloud'.

Why do I have my computer read it?

Our brains often 'fill in the blanks' because we know what we meant, but that doesn't help us find typos, and spellcheckers are of no use when you type the word *'he'* instead of *'the'* or *'then'* instead of *'than'* because it's not misspelled, it's the wrong word.

For the *he/the* example, listening to your computer read it will help you find that error, but when it comes to *then/than*, they sound so similar that you might not hear the difference. For words that sound the same but are spelled differently, Grammarly will help you find and fix those mistakes, as well as other common errors that sound the same such as *there/their/they're*, *you're/your*, *here/hear*, and *to/two/too* to name but a few.

With the exception of those types of errors, the computer reading your book to you does help you fast-track proofreading because it cannot 'fill in the blanks' like your brain can... the computer can only read what is actually written. If you used the wrong word in a sentence, you'll probably hear it.

It's worth noting that it does take a bit of time to get used to the sound of computer-generated speech, also known as TTS. My copy of Microsoft Word comes with three voices: David, Zira and Mark. I find the Zira voice to be the easiest to listen to for an extended period of time.

As a side note:

When using programs such as Grammarly or the editor that comes with Microsoft Word, <u>don't assume they are correct</u>. You need to read the entire sentence to make sure the grammar checker you are using didn't make the mistake of suggesting the wrong word. It happens quite frequently because grammar checkers are far from perfect, and they can never replace human editors.

SOMETIMES YOU JUST HAVE TO KILL A TREE

My favorite 'trick', and the one I always recommend, even if you use TTS voices, is to print a copy of your book and then read it... out loud.

The 'out loud' part is important because no matter how many times you read what you wrote off your computer screen, as soon as you read it out loud from a piece of paper, you'll find even more typos.

An added bonus to using paper, aside from being able to quickly highlight any errors you find, is you can easily write ideas and editing remarks in the margins and then continue proofreading your book. If you only proofread on your computer and start fixing mistakes right away, you'll often find yourself rewriting certain sections instead of proofreading.

So my method, in a nutshell, is to brainstorm ideas to index cards or mind mapping software, write the book based off those index cards, let the computer read it to me to listen for mistakes, use Grammarly to find and fix typos I missed, then print it and read it out loud.

Once those steps are completed and the typos are fixed to the best of my abilities, I get my computer to read it a second time, from start to finish.

Each time I rewrite something I get the computer to read that section followed by another round of Grammarly edits until I think the book is done. Then I have the computer read it to me one last time, from the very beginning to the very end, to make sure it sounds good as a whole.

Once all those steps are completed and the book is the best I can possibly make it, I then send the updated draft to my beta readers for their input.

Author's Note:

Why do I have the computer read it to find mistakes when I have to use Grammarly anyway because typos on words like *there, they're* or *their* will be missed, creating an extra step? Wouldn't it make more sense just to use Grammarly in the first place?

Yes and No.

Allow me to explain…

First, my eyesight is not what it used to be. Constantly staring at a computer screen is tiring, so having my computer read it to me allows me to proofread the book for more common mistakes without having to really focus on a computer screen.

Plus, I suffer from back pain *(as opposed to enjoying back pain; which is why 'I suffer from' always sounded like a weird expression to me.)* Having the computer read it to me not only creates less eye strain, but I can stand up and walk around while I am listening. I also have a 'desk riser' that raises my laptop to the correct height while standing so I can quickly edit mistakes without having to bend down to type.

Secondly, and even more importantly, how something sounds when we read it 'in our head' as opposed to hearing it out loud are two different things.

How a sentence is structured may 'sound' okay to us when we read it in our head, but once you hear it out loud, it sometimes sounds a bit 'off' if not confusing. Having my computer read it to me allows me to just listen to how it 'flows' so I can fix any issues I hear with sentence structure.

While it is true that eventually I will be reading it out loud myself, just hearing your words spoken by someone else, even if that 'someone else' is a computer-generated voice, really does make a difference. That, and my printed document will have less mistakes to fix because my computer helped me catch a lot of them right away before I printed it.

Even though I highly recommend printing and reading your book out loud, it can be a bit of a pain switching back and forth between looking at your computer and all your notes and the typos you highlighted on paper. Finding and fixing as many mistakes as you can before you print it saves you a lot of back-and-forth between paper and your computer screen.

YOUR FIRST DRAFT SUCKS!

There, I said it.

No matter how great you think your book is when you finished your first draft, it really isn't… it needs a lot of work.

Never publish your first draft!

The first draft is for your eyes only. It's only after you proofread and edited it a couple of times will your book really start to take shape.

It is only when you edit your book until you think it is perfect and you can't possibly make it any better do you send it to beta readers for their input so they can help you polish it even more!

One of the biggest mistakes first-time authors make is believing their first draft is as good as their family and friends tell them it is.

It's not.

They are just being nice so as not to hurt your feelings.

The screenshot below is an actual book published on Amazon and is a great example as to why **you should never publish your first draft,** and at the very least you need beta readers (which we will cover in the next section) who will offer constructive criticism so you don't publish something like this:

22 year old sian strolled along the cobbled streets of london her curly red hair blowing gently in the wind out of the corner of her eye sian saw a man who she thought was someone she dreamnt about the night before

sian - (to herslef) this really cant be happening

the short guy with the medium length blonde hair walked fast past the crowd not skipping a beat

The author *(who is someone I know and gave me permission to include a screenshot of his book)* refused to make any changes because as he said, "I like what I wrote." His family and friends all said they liked it too and that was good enough for him, so he published his first draft… mistakes and all!

Everyone's First Draft Sucks - And So Does Yours! Don't believe the hype and false praise by people who only want to stroke your ego by being nice. They're not doing you any favors!

BETA READERS

While I do not recommend using family or friends to edit your book, getting some feedback from them can help **if you can convince them to be honest with you and offer constructive criticism** rather than just stroking your ego.

A good beta reader is someone who reads your finished draft and then makes detailed notes about what they liked or disliked about your book.

As mentioned, family members and friends can be helpful, but they do not typically make the best readers because they often give you false praise so as not to hurt your feelings.

If you only go by what they say, you'll jump to the next phase of the publishing process without making any changes, and no matter how good you think your book is, or how good your family and friends say it is, it's not ready to be published.

When that person sent me a copy of his manuscript, I tried to talk him out of publishing it to no avail. As you witnessed in the small section that I grabbed a screenshot of, there are plenty of mistakes that could have been easily fixed.

There isn't any punctuation to speak of, he didn't use any capitalization, and throughout his manuscript he frequently used Messenger/Facebook-style words like 'ur' instead of 'you are' and 'i no' instead of 'I know' and several others that made his book barely legible.

Of course, as I mentioned, **his family and friends all said they thought it was great, and he made the mistake of believing them**.

When I asked him how many times he rewrote his book to finetune it and make it better, I was not surprised when he said that he never rewrote any of it.

Never do that.

As I mentioned, I tried to talk him out of publishing it, but he was having no part of that because his family and friends all thought it was great, and that was good enough for him. So he published his first draft… mistakes and all.

Needless to say, he doesn't get any sales to speak of. Once people use the "Look Inside" feature and see just how poorly it was written, they quickly move on to something else because no one, other than family and friends who want to support him, wants to buy a book that looks like it was haphazardly thrown together by someone who is barely literate.

My apologies if that sounds harsh, but things like spelling and grammar matter.

You may get away with it on Facebook, and some people have been known to jump in and defend poorly written posts by labeling anyone who dares speak up as 'the grammar police' (as if having good grammar and knowing how to spell should be shunned) but in the publishing world, readers expect more… a lot more.

If they are going to give you their time and money, they expect you not to waste it. So use every tool at your disposal to make sure it's your best work, and that includes using beta readers who will be honest with you.

Finding good beta readers is not that difficult.

Just about every town has at least one writing group. Your local library is often a great resource because people who write books are usually avid readers. If you live in a small town and can't find a writing group, start your own. Chances are your local library will even let you use their facilities to host the group meetings.

Manuscript swapping with other authors, whether local or from an online group, is a great way to find beta readers who will give you honest feedback in exchange for beta reading their book and offering feedback in return.

This comes with one, very important caveat...

Only exchange manuscripts with people who are writing books in a different genre or topic than you. If you give your *'How-to Lose 10 Pounds Diet and Exercise Book'* to someone who is also writing a diet and exercise book, you run the risk of having them steal some of your ideas... or blame you for stealing their ideas.

Many times, the people you are exchanging manuscripts with are not known to you personally, and you have no idea who or what they are really like. In this case, I urge you to first copyright protect your book with the U.S. Copyright Office (www.copyright.gov), or whatever copyright office is available for your country, before sending your manuscript to beta readers.

Remember that beta reading is not to tear someone's book apart; it is to help them find things they overlooked to make their book even stronger.

In the case of fiction, it is often finding plot holes that the author missed because they were too close to their story, and frequently it is helping them finetune their dialog and character arcs.

For nonfiction, it is often discovering that some sections are too complicated, or the author was unintentionally talking down to the reader.

It's a fine line, and a neutral third-party beta reader will find them a lot quicker, and more honestly, than your family and friends who want to support your writing efforts.

If your beta reader only says something like *"I liked it, it was really good"* but didn't explain why they liked it or what parts they found good, it's best to thank them for their time and then move on to the next beta reader; they have to tell you what they liked or disliked about it and why, or else they're not really telling you anything of value, and are often just stroking your ego.

Yes, it feels good to hear positive praise, that's why you get your mom and grandma to read it, but you didn't ask a beta reader to read your book to make you feel good; you asked them because you want constructive criticism to make your book even better.

WHEN TO IGNORE BETA READERS

It is always best to ask several people to read your book to get a variety of feedback, but just because your beta reader says there is something wrong with one or more parts of your book, other than a typo that you missed, you don't have to change it. **You can't please everyone; nor should you try.**

If you have five beta readers but only one of them has an issue with something, it's probably safe to ignore that comment and move on because no one else had an issue with it. However, if several of them tell you that a certain part of your book is just not working, such as being too vague or you are over-explaining something, chances are you need to change it.

When all is said and done, it's your book; if you feel strongly about something you don't have to change anything if you don't want to… just make sure it is not your ego talking that's making you refuse to make changes.

If several people have the same issue about something, then it's most likely an issue that needs to be addressed.

Put your ego aside and fix it!

If they found an issue with it, chances are your readers, the ones who purchased your book, will have the same issue.

You need a thick skin to take constructive criticism because first-time writers often feel like it's a personal attack against them.

It's not.

Your beta readers are not trying to hurt your feelings, they are trying to help you, so let them.

You have to leave your ego at the door and fix problems. If you don't, you'll most likely end up with poor reviews, and that in turn will hurt your sales because the people who spent their hard-earned money to buy your book are not worried about hurting your feelings.

They're not being mean; they are just being honest.

It's better to get that honesty upfront from your beta readers than it is in the form of bad reviews.

Part 3 - Book Covers

I'm a fan of DIY and usually create the entire book myself, including the cover; other times I have someone else design the cover for me. It depends entirely on what book I am working on and whether or not I am satisfied with the cover I created.

It's worth noting that I've spent a great deal of time over the years designing posters, flyers, and other materials for huge companies and local non-profits, so I have some design experience.

When you hire a cover designer, you have to give up the reins on your cover art to some extent. Of course, you can and should use your gut instinct (which is often correct) to determine when a cover is right for your book, but chances are the designer will have better ideas because it is after all, what they do.

I know of a few people who hire a designer and then tell them exactly what to do. Not what they want, not sharing their initial thoughts and then letting the designer come up with something based off their ideas… they told the designer *exactly* how they want their cover to look. This never made sense to me because if the designer is only allowed to do exactly what the author says, why did they waste their money paying a designer? Just do it yourself, because the designer is not allowed to design anything anyways.

The image, the fonts and the colors are just some of the design elements needed to create a worthwhile cover. Readers in your niche, the people who buy books, have certain expectations. Your designer is familiar with them (well, they should be if the designer is any good) and they know how to create a cover that not only stands out, but helps you sell your book because here's the cold, hard truth that many first-time writers do not want to hear…

Nobody cares about you or your book!

Not yet.

They are not buying your book to help you or because you spent a great deal of time working on it; they buy books because they need a problem solved. **You either have the answer, or you don't… it really is that simple.** They care about results.

If your book doesn't provide the answers they are looking for or fill their desire, do you honestly think they care that you worked so hard on writing a book that is of no use to them?

The answer of course, is no.

As I said, they don't care about you or your book, they care about their needs, not yours. It is only after you have supplied them with the help they need will they start to care about you.

So why would they buy your book if they don't care about you?

Because **people really do judge a book by its cover**.

With dozens or hundreds of books to choose from in your niche, your book has to stand out from the crowd. It is only AFTER your book cover grabs their attention will they flip it over to read the back matter to see if the book will be to their liking or, in the case of Amazon, click the 'Look Inside' option to read more about the book.

Great covers get them to flip it over or look inside. Great covers are not a fluke; they are created by great cover designers.

Editing your book's content, recording it as an audiobook, and book covers are the three areas where I recommend you hire someone else to do the work rather than attempting it yourself, especially when you first start out.

When looking for a cover designer, know that the chances of you finding a great designer on sites like *Fivver* is highly unlikely. Covers cost money, and five bucks simply won't get you a great cover.

You have to be able to work with your designer. This means you tell them what ideas you have (if any) and let them run with it, and you have the right to request changes that doesn't feel right to you. Remember, they are the designer and usually know best, but you know your book. If something doesn't feel right, you reserve the right to make changes because you're the one who has to live with the results.

Don't be afraid to ask for samples of work they have done. Looking at a selection of mock covers is <u>not</u> work they have done. Yes, mock covers can give you an idea of what they are capable of, but some less-than-honorable 'designers' have been known to display the work of other designers to lure people into hiring them, and the author finds out after they paid their hard-earned money that the designer cannot deliver.

Looking at actual books they have designed helps you separate real designers from the fake ones. Be sure to look up the book on sites like Amazon and use the 'Look Inside' feature to see if their name is listed as the cover designer. You could also contact the author and ask them what it was like to work with that designer.

It's always best to get as much information up front so you'll have a better idea of what to expect.

If you see a book cover you really like, find out if there is a way to contact the author and ask them who their designer was. If they are happy with their designer, then chances are they'll be more than happy to tell you because they'll want to pay it forward.

If there was a problem, they'll tell you that too.

It's best to stick to self-published authors for this because mainstream authors from major publishing houses are not readily available to answer questions from first-time writers, or there is no way to contact them directly because they receive mountains of fan mail. Even if they were willing to answer your questions, it could be months before they even get around to reading your email, and the cost of their designer is probably outside your budget anyways.

It doesn't hurt to ask indie authors about their cover because you're considering hiring their designer, just **don't ask them to read your manuscript**. Most are too busy working on their latest book to read unsolicited manuscripts from someone they've never heard of.

Over time, when you have built a relationship with that author, some of them are willing to help their fellow indie authors but asking for favors from them right out of the gate is frowned upon. But simply asking who their cover designer is should be okay.

The worst that can happen is they don't answer you; the worst that can happen if you don't do your due diligence is you end up with a less-than-professional who does shoddy work or takes you for an expensive ride.

When you hire a cover designer, it's a good idea to tell them that you want both covers created. It's a lot easier, and less expensive, to have both covers created upfront than to rehire the designer a second time.

I have worked with and highly recommend Luke Romyn as a cover designer. He has created covers for both my fiction and non-fiction books, including this one. I can't say enough good things about him. You can contact him at: www.lukeromyn.com

On the next page are just a few of the covers Luke has created.

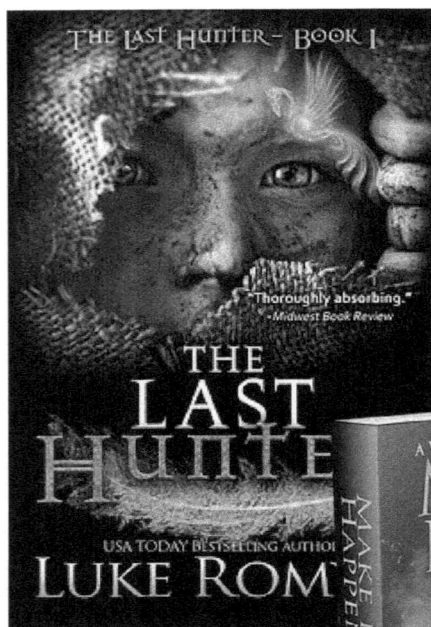

THE LAST HUNTER – BOOK I

"Thoroughly absorbing."
-Midwest Book Review

THE LAST HUNTER

USA TODAY BESTSELLING AUTHOR
LUKE ROM

USA TODAY BESTSELLING AUTHOR
LUKE ROMYN

BLACKLISTED

COMES AT A PRICE.

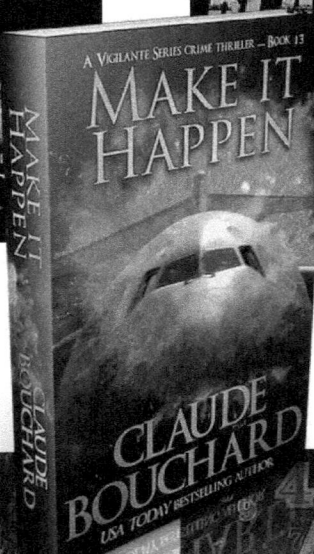

A VIGILANTE SERIES CRIME THRILLER – BOOK 13
MAKE IT HAPPEN

CLAUDE BOUCHARD
USA TODAY BESTSELLING AUTHOR

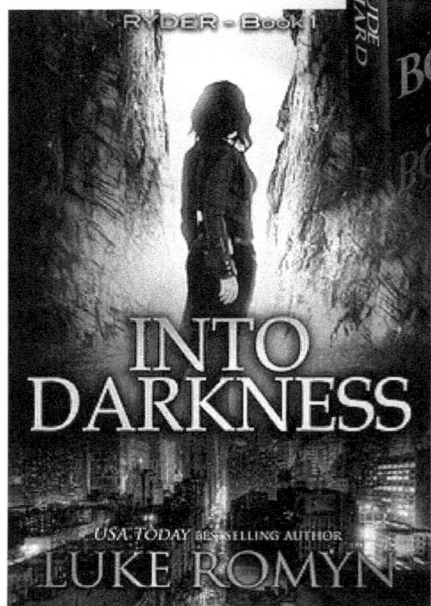

RYDER – Book I

INTO DARKNESS

USA TODAY BESTSELLING AUTHOR
LUKE ROMYN

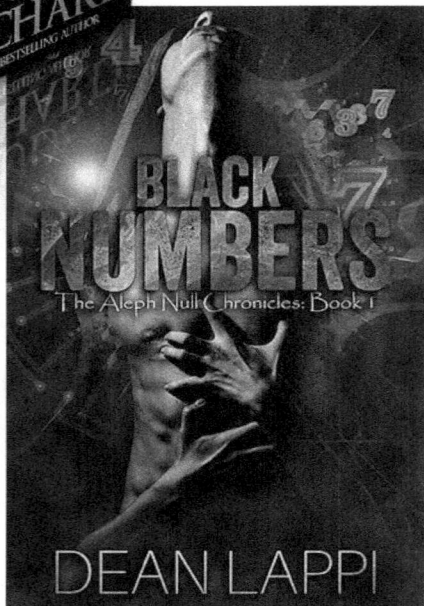

BLACK NUMBERS
The Aleph Null Chronicles: Book I

DEAN LAPPI

WHERE TO FIND IMAGES FOR BOOK COVERS

Canva (www.canva.com) seems to be the go-to place for indie authors to find images for creating covers. Pexels.com, Pixabay.com and similar sites are also popular for finding images.

The important thing to remember when using those or any site is to **never assume that you have the right to use the image for your book** just because you found it on that site. Many times, they also host images by ShutterStock (for example) as a way to help pay for their site. You cannot use Shutterstock (and similar images) for free, which means you need to verify that the image itself (not just the site) is a public domain image and/or is licensed for commercial use, not just personal use. Once you upload your book to Amazon or any other site, you are now using their image for commercial purposes.

"Royalty Free" is not the same as "Public Domain."

Public domain could mean that the copyright expired or it could also mean that the original creator has 'given up their rights' to their work. Some creators do this as a way of 'paying it forward' so that other people can use their photograph or graphic art without paying for it and without given any type of credit.

Images that have been released as Royalty Free or with a Creative Commons license often have certain stipulations. These stipulations could mean several things such as: giving proper credit (exactly the way they want it written) in your book and/or marketing materials, or that you can freely use the image but you cannot modify it in any way, or maybe you are required to pay a one-time fee for the rights to use the image.

Yes, giving credit where credit is due is a good thing, but if *how* they want you to list that credit in your book and/or marketing materials is not to your liking, or if it distracts from your content, then public domain is often the best way to go.

I use public domain images for exactly that reason…

Giving artists proper credit on a page in the book itself is one thing and I'm more than happy to do it, but if I have to list that credit on everything I make, that creates an issue for me because I do not want to link to their website every time I create a promo video or book trailer with that image - the only link I want viewers to see in the promo video or book trailer is MY link so they can purchase my book, not the link to the website of the person who created the image.

IMPORTANT: Always do a Google Search to see if, and how, others are using the image you are considering for your book.

You cannot *'stand out from the crowd'* when several other books all have the same cover image. It is a public domain image… that means **if you thought it would make a great book cover, so have other people**.

There are bound to be some duplicates either now or in the future, but that's the chance you take when you do not take the picture yourself or hire a photographer for completely original cover art.

I once found an image of a teen girl that reminded me of the main character in my middle-grade novel. Someone had taken the original photograph and made her appear 'ghostly.' Because my middle-grade book was a ghost story, it would have been perfect.

Except for one very important detail…

When I did a Google search for that image, I discovered that several porn-related sites used the original photograph to attract visitors. There was nothing distasteful about the image nor was it sexualized in any way, it was just the image of a pretty girl, but some porn sites will use any picture they can find to try and get more traffic.

Obviously, the very last thing I wanted was the cover of my children's book showing up in search results next to porn sites, so that cover idea was deleted and I continued my search.

Always do a Google search of the image you plan on using to make sure that how other people are using that image will not shine a negative light on you and your book.

AMAZON'S COVER CREATOR

It's worth noting that Amazon offers a free, online cover creator, but I do not recommend using it because you'll probably end up with an unprofessional looking cover, especially if you don't have any design experience.

Most readers can spot those inferior covers and typically skip over those books because they know that an unprofessional cover on the outside means the inside, the actual content, is equally as unprofessional, and not worth their time or money.

People really do judge a book by the cover.

In the next section we'll go over some basic formatting for paperbacks. Even if your original plan is only to publish an ebook, it's a good idea to have both a paperback and an ebook available because it increases your chances of getting more sales.

Plus, physical books make great gifts.

Part 4 – Book Formatting

In this section we will go over book formatting to help you generate more sales by having both a paperback and ebook available for the buying public.

The most popular size for paperbacks on Amazon by independently published authors is 6" x 9". This is the size you should strive for unless your book has very specific requirements, such as the pages need to be larger for recipes, a photobook, a calendar, and so on.

In your word processor, go into your page settings to make the following changes because most new documents start with the standard 8 ½ x 11 or A4 page with one-inch margins and no gutter.

For this section I will be using Microsoft Word.

In a new document, go to the LAYOUT TAB. You can then select the little dropdown arrow to the right of the words 'page setup' to open the popup. If you do not see this, simply select MARGINS then CUSTOM MARGINS.

Change the top, bottom, inside, and outside margins to .25" (point twenty-five inches). Next, change the gutter size to .375" (point three hundred and seventy-five inches). **These are the typical settings for most 6" x 9" paperbacks from 100 to 200 pages.** Your version of Word may change the gutter to .38, which is perfectly fine.

Depending on your book's length, you may require a larger (or smaller) gutter size and margins. We'll discuss that in more detail a little later. For now, those margins will suffice.

Amazon does have a tool to help you determine the exact sizes you need, but here's the thing…. that only works when your book is complete and you know how many pages your 6x9 book is, which you can never figure out when you are typing to the default 8 ½ by 11-inch or A4 document. Plus, those margins and gutter sizes will most likely change as you write and edit your book, which can add or subtract pages, so you may have to tweak the margins and maybe even the gutter size a couple of times to get it exactly right.

Rather than going through all that guess work, just select the margins and the gutter size I recommended above - you'll at least be in the right ballpark.

Below that, under 'Multiple Pages', select 'Mirrored Margins.'

What this essentially means is that the pages on the left will have the gutter on the right, the pages on the right will have the gutter on the left. This is needed for physical books because the pages have to be glued together, and you don't want the text set too close to the spine or it makes reading the text more difficult, and you have to bend the pages back a little more to clearly see the text, which causes undo wear and tear on the spine.

Next, select the PAPER tab. Change the width to 6" and the height to 9".

Next select the LAYOUT tab.

Place a check mark in the options for *"Different Odd and Even"* and *"Different First Page."* Your first page is your Title page and you don't want page numbers etc. on it.

If you wish to have the even pages display your name with the page number, and the odd pages to display your book's title with the page number, or you want the page numbers to be justified all the way to the left and right, the 'Different Even and Odd Pages' option takes care of that for you. If you just want basic page numbering that are not justified left and right (that is, the page numbers are always centered at the top or bottom of the page) uncheck the 'Different Even and Odd Pages' option.

All the other settings should be fine for most books.

Select OK to save your settings which will also exit you out of the settings popup.

You are now ready to start writing.

Time Saving Tip:

> Now that you created a blank document with the proper page size, margins, and gutter for most books that you will be writing, it's a good idea to first select SAVE AS and name it something like: "My Book Template" and save it to your hard drive. Then select SAVE AS again, only this time save it with your book's actual title. From that point on, every time you save the document it'll be with your book's title, and the template will remain untouched.

> When you are ready to write a new book, you don't have to go through the setup steps again to reset the size and margins; you simply open the "My Book Template", do another SAVE AS with your new books title, and you're off and running.

Now that you are ready to start writing your book, the first thing you type is the title of your book. Press ENTER and type your name, then press ENTER again.

That's it; that is your basic title page.

You can play with the fonts, sizes and position later, for now, we're just typing our first draft.

Don't spend too much time thinking of what the best title should be for your book. Any title will do for now because you can always change it later. Your focus should be on getting your first draft done, so don't stress over minor details.

If you can't come up with a title, just call it *"My Book"* and move on. As you write and think about your book, that great title will come to you.

If it's a 'How-to book', for now just call it "How to ____" and fill in what the main topic of your book is, such as *How To Scrapbook, How To Plan a Wedding Without Losing Your Mind, How To Lose 10 Pounds*, or whatever your How-to book is about.

As you write, remember that you really don't have to worry about spelling or grammar either; just write.

The quote I tell first-time writers that sums this up nicely is from the movie *'Finding Forrester'* starring Sean Connery:

> *"You must write your first draft with your heart. You rewrite with your head. The first key to writing is... to write, not to think."*

Rewrites are for fixing typos and finding better ways to get your ideas across. The first draft is basically an info dump; getting your ideas out of your head and on the page. **It's also why you never publish your first draft.**

I keep repeating that sentence because it really is that important. Too many first-time authors fall in love with their first draft and don't want to change it.

That is a mistake, but it's one you can easily avoid.

Next, Hold the CTRL key (Control key on a PC) and press ENTER again. This inserts a page break so the next thing you type will be on a new page in your Word document. You don't want to repeatedly hit Enter to bring the cursor to a new page because when you later change the text during rewrites, those extra line breaks will be pushed down the page and onto the next page, which means everything you wanted to start at the top of a new page will also be pushed down. So to keep the start of each new chapter or section on the top of a new page, always use this handy shortcut (CTRL-ENTER) to quickly insert a clean page break.

From there you start writing your book's content according to the chapter headings and subheadings that you created on your index cards or in your mind-mapping software.

The other reason I suggested that you create the margins first is so that you always have a visual representation that approximates what the finished book will look like. If paragraphs are broken across pages, or if an accompanying picture or graphic gets bumped to the next page, you'll be able to see what is happening in your document as you write, and you can make minor adjustments as needed during the editing phase.

As mentioned, don't worry about this as you write your first draft; just get the information out of your head and on the page and worry about formatting and moving things around during the editing stage to make your book look even better. And one of the best ways to do that is to start with a 6x9 document with the proper margins. Just remember that once you have finished writing and proofreading your book, you may have to change those margins and possibly the gutter size before you upload it to Amazon.

You do this by reading your book again while keeping an eye on whether or not a paragraph is broken across two pages (which may or may not be what you want) and if the accompanying pictures or graphics (if any) are inadvertently pushed to the next page.

Most times, in nonfiction books, having the image on the same page as the description is preferred so the reader can easily switch back and forth between the text and the image to get a better understanding of what you are explaining without having to physically turn the page back and forth.

If the text is on the left page and the image is on the right, that is perfectly fine because your readers can see both - it's when the text is on the right page and the accompanying image is on the next page, readers have to physically turn the page to see the graphic, then turn the page back again to finish reading the explainer text.

It is worth noting that it is the 'little things' like re-reading your book several times to make sure the margins and gutter sizes work as expected, and that the images or graphics are positioned properly are why some people never finish their book… it's too much 'work' reading their own book over and over every time they make major changes… it is not difficult, but it is time consuming.

It is the little things like paying attention to these types of details is where many people give up, or they just don't bother, which means their book is less than great. It may not seem like much, but it's those little details that separate great books from the less-than-impressive books being sold by independent authors.

I have read books where the chapter heading was on one page and the first paragraph started on the next page, or the image wasn't centered properly, or a couple of words were printed next to the image but then the next sentence was below the image, which gave the book a less-than-professional look.

You do not have a lot of control over this in ebooks because the user's personal settings will change the fonts sizes, but there are no excuses for printed books other than laziness or just not caring.

If you are the type of person who likes to edit on paper, and I recommend you do it at least once, you may prefer to skip this section for now since you will be printing to standard 8.5 x 11 or A4 paper.

I personally just print it using the 6x9 setup because it's really not that many pages in the difference; the benefits of writing in 6x9 with the proper margins and gutter size far outweigh the few extra pages needed to print it (and printer paper is relatively cheap.) I should point out that I reuse the paper by printing on the opposite, blank side for the next round of edits before it goes into the shredder to be recycled.

If by some chance you only want to publish ebooks and not paperbacks, you don't have to set a gutter size because ebooks do not require them.

FONTS MATTER

For printed books, Times New Roman style fonts are often preferred because they look better and cause less eye strain. If you are reading the paperback version of this book, the main text is done in Palatino Linotype, 12-point font.

Ebooks typically look better using Arial or **Verdana**-style fonts because they cause the least amount of eye strain. The end-user's Kindle or ebook software may change the font and size depending on their personal settings.

Do not use any of the *script* or handwriting fonts because they are very difficult to read for many people, and **Comic Sans** type fonts look unprofessional.

It's best to only use one or two fonts in your book.

A CASE STUDY OF WHAT NOT TO DO

A few years ago, a self-published author wanted to hire me to turn his novel into a screenplay. When he described the story, it sounded like it would make a good movie so I agreed to read his book, but when I received a copy in the mail, I quickly discovered just how difficult it would be to work with that book to turn it into a screenplay.

For starters, the author used different fonts and different fonts sizes for each character, making his book look very amateurish.

He also made the mistake of using language that the average person would not understand, which meant they would need to keep a dictionary close by just to figure out what the heck the author was saying.

This typically happens when first-time writers spend too much time looking up words in a thesaurus to make their book sound more impressive, but here's the thing: that can, and usually does, backfire. A thesaurus is a great tool if used sparingly, but chances are, when you look a word up in a thesaurus, the word you were originally going to use is often the best word to use anyway.

Another problem with his book that often plagues beginner writers, is making the mistake of trying to sound more intelligent by using big, impressive words that the average reader doesn't understand. Using 'ten-dollar words' serves no purpose other than the author showing off and stroking their own ego.

The author didn't even include any page numbers in his novel, which I estimated was over 450 pages. It would take over twelve hours to read a 450-page book in one sitting which most people can't or won't do. If I lost my place when I put the book down, I had to guess where I left off by re-reading pages until I found my spot again. What a horrible thing to do to your readers!

You may think your book is a page-turner that most people won't be able to put down, but here's another cold, hard truth that many first-time writers do not want to hear:

If you didn't use beta readers or never hired an editor to help you polish your manuscript, it's not nearly as good as you think it is, and it needs <u>a lot</u> of work!

Sorry, but that's just the way it is.

It takes time to find and develop your writing voice; you can't do that with your very first book!

The author in this case study couldn't have done either of those things because somebody would have pointed out those problems, such as all the weird fonts and font sizes, the lack of page numbers, and all those ten-dollar words that the average person wouldn't understand to name but a few of the issues I found with his novel.

Or maybe he did use them, but he just ignored their advice because in his mind, his manuscript was the greatest thing ever written… if those people couldn't see his genius then they didn't know what they were talking about!

Sadly, that's a common tale.

Unfortunately, what I did manage to read did not make a lot of sense to me. Of course, there's always the chance that I was just being too critical and maybe it wasn't really that bad, so I asked my fiancé, an avid reader, to read it to get her thoughts on it. She read less than a dozen pages before she gave up and said that it was giving her a headache.

Eventually I had to tell the author that I simply could not read his book and as such, I was not interested in turning it into a screenplay. It just wasn't worth it.

Of course, the author argued the point and told me I was wrong because so many people loved his story. He then told me that he was a taxi driver, and he always had a few copies of his novel in the taxi with him; when he picked people up at the airport, he would give them a copy of his book to read on the long drive back.

According to him, most of his passengers told him how great his book was so he did not understand why I wouldn't jump at the chance to turn it into a screenplay.

Like many first-time authors, he made the unfortunate mistake of believing anyone who said what he wanted to hear, and anyone who did not like his masterpiece was wrong.

At one point in the conversation, he admitted that of all the passengers he let read his novel, he only sold a small handful of books, which begs the question…

If all his passengers thought his book was so great, why didn't they buy it?

Because, just like family members and friends that you get to read your book, they want to support your writing efforts and are being nice so as not to hurt your feelings.

If those passengers honestly thought the book was great, they would have jumped at the chance to buy a copy directly off the author, because they could also get it signed on the spot.

But the majority of them didn't buy it.

Maybe they were just being nice because it would have made for a long, uncomfortable drive if they told him the truth. It would be a lot easier, and less awkward, to just give false praise so as not to hurt his feelings than having to explain why you did not like his book.

I'm glad he was able to sell the copies that he did, and I have to admit, letting passengers in your cab read your book is actually a brilliant idea because on those long drives you have a captive audience… learning that their cabbie is also a writer is definitely more interesting than talking about the weather or about the flight, and it certainly is a great way to sell more books, but you have to have a book worth buying.

The main take-away from this case study…

Numbers don't lie. If a lot of people read the opening chapters of your book but do not buy it to finish reading it, it doesn't matter how much praise they give you… if they don't buy your book, there is something wrong with it that needs to be fixed.

False praise serves no purpose but to stroke your ego. Honesty and constructive criticism sometimes hurt, but just remember that it's not a personal attack against you… they are being honest to help you make your book even better, so pay attention to what they are saying.

AMAZON'S PRINT SIZE CALCULATOR

As mentioned, Amazon has a free tool you can use to get precise measurements of your paperback's interior and cover.

The tool is actually an Excel Macro-Enabled Worksheet; when you enter the trim size (such as 6 x 9), the ink and type of paper (black interior on cream paper) and how many pages your book is, the tool automatically determines what the gutter and margins should be for books with or without bleed (we'll cover that in a future chapter), as well as the trim sizes for the cover.

It's fairly straightforward to use, and Amazon has plenty of help files if needed.

Just remember that every time you adjust the margins and/or gutter, review your entire manuscript again so there won't be any formatting surprises.

Another thing to keep in mind is when you exit the spreadsheet it'll ask you if you want to save the file. There is really no need to do this since every time you use it you want to start with a clean slate, so you can safely exit it without saving the changes so it doesn't "mess anything up" the next time you need to use it.

Making minor tweaks to your book that adds or removes an extra page shouldn't create any issues, but sometimes the formatting could be thrown out of whack with even the smallest of changes, so it's always best to verify your book's interior is EXACTLY the way you want it, then save the Word document to make sure you have the latest changes saved to your hard drive, then export it as a PDF.

Use this link to download Amazon's FREE Paperback file setup calculator to get precise measurements of your paperback's interior and cover:

https://kenncrawford.com/amazontool

Part 5 – Amazon KDP

All the steps necessary to upload a book to Amazon KDP is beyond the scope of this book, but I included this section because there is something you should know when it comes to uploading your manuscript to Amazon, and that is what format to use.

The following is from KDP's support documents:

> *PDFs are ideal for paperbacks, and they are required if your manuscript contains elements that bleed.*
>
> *However, PDFs don't always convert well to eBooks. You can create a separate file to upload for your eBook, or, if your manuscript doesn't contain bleed, you can use the same manuscript file for both your paperback and eBook. Format it in DOC (.doc), DOCX (.docx), HTML (.html), or RTF (.rtf) for best results.*

The first five words in that support text are the most important ones to remember:

"PDFs are ideal for paperbacks."

I have uploaded manuscripts that I saved as a Microsoft document (.docx) which is an acceptable format, but when I used the book previewer (a necessary step in the book creation process in KDP) I found some of the formatting wasn't exactly how I created it in the original document.

However, when I exported the exact same document to a PDF file, then uploaded that to KDP, it was always exactly the way I wanted it to look in the book previewer.

From that point on, **I only upload PDFs for the paperback version** of my books.

For Kindle ebooks, it's a different matter entirely. I recommend using their KDP Kindle Creator software to create the necessary files. You'll learn more about that in the next section but first, remember what I said about *it's the little things that count*?

During the KDP book creation process, one of the steps is the 'book previewer.' **Never assume the book converted properly even if you uploaded a PDF**. Take the time to review each and every page in the KDP previewer to make sure that something doesn't get pushed to the next page or that your formatting wasn't thrown out of whack during the conversion process.

It does take a bit of time to flip through each page in the previewer <u>for the entire book</u> to verify the formatting is correct, but it is these little 'time consuming' steps that many first-time writers don't bother to do, which results in publishing a less than perfect book when it could have been easily avoided.

As I've mentioned a few times already: **if you don't care about your book, nobody else will either.**

KINDLE CREATE EBOOK CREATION SOFTWARE

Kindle Create is a free interior formatting tool that works well with most books you want to publish on Amazon. How to use the software is outside the scope of this guide, but Amazon has plenty of help files to assist you.

Use this link to download the latest version of Kindle Create for your PC or Mac computer:

https://kenncrawford.com/kindlecreate

Kindle Create has professionally designed themes with chapter titles, drop caps, and image placement options to make your ebook look its very best, and with the Kindle Previewer, you see exactly what your readers will see.

The important thing to remember is Kindle Create only uses .doc or .docx files, not PDFs, .html or .rtf files, which is why I suggested you save the latest version of your book as a Word doc, and then export it as a PDF, so you'll have both versions readily available to create the paperback and ebook versions of your book.

STAYING ORGANIZED

Every time I make major changes to the book I am working on, I do a SAVE AS and give it a new filename in sequential order, such as:

MyBookTitle001, MyBookTitle002, MyBookTitle003 and so on.

NEVER keep overwriting the same file when you make major changes! If at some point during the editing process you decide that an earlier version was better, you can always go back to that previous version, then copy/paste the section you want into your current manuscript.

If you just kept resaving the same document over and over again, you cannot go back to a previous version, which means you have to rewrite it from scratch and hope you remember exactly what and how you wrote that section.

Yes, you can use CTRL-Z to undo what you typed, but if you did a lot of editing and then decided that something from an earlier section of the book was better, you would have to undo all the changes you wanted to keep just to get back to that other section (and that's if your software can handle that many undo actions.)

It's a lot easier to just do a SAVE AS with a new filename each time you make changes so you can grab an earlier section from anywhere in the previous drafts without undoing everything you have edited in the current version.

This does create a fair amount of files on your hard drive, but Word documents are not very large. This book is less than 5 megs (megabytes) in size; I could save over 200 versions and only use around 1 GB (gigabyte) of hard drive space. It's worth noting that I only do a 'Save As' for major changes, not every single time I save a copy.

Speaking of: Click Save to Save Your Sanity…

Computer crashes and power outages happen at the most inconvenient of times. Even if your word processor is setup to automatically save a backup file, I recommend hitting 'save' every 10 minutes, and uploading a backup copy to an external drive or to the cloud every 30 minutes. That way, if something does go wrong, you only lose a few minutes work.

If you don't make a habit of regularly saving your work, you could end up losing hours of writing. It's just not worth the risk when it only takes one or two seconds to click 'save.'

I also keep one copy on my hard drive, a second copy on an external drive, and I upload a third copy to the cloud (such as OneDrive or Google Drive.) I do this in case my hard drive crashes. If it does, I don't lose all my hard work because it is also saved in two other places.

It's also worth noting that when I have the final draft that is ready to be published, I save it twice. First, I do a SAVE AS with the word FINAL in the title, then I do a SAVE AS again and give it a new name, such as "INTERIOR – My Book Title", and I save my cover as "COVER – My Book Title".

The reason for this is because I have so many versions saved to the book's folder, I don't want to accidentally upload the wrong version (I've done that) or upload the cover to the manuscript section and the manuscript to the cover section (I've done that before too.) So, I got into the habit of ONLY uploading the files that start with the word INTERIOR or COVER so I always know what file to upload and to where.

It seems rather silly and redundant to do it that way but believe me, when you are going through the various steps to upload your book, you can easily make a mistake, which slows down the uploading process.

I have a separate folder created for each book I am working on, and to keep things even more organized, I create a new folder within the book's folder called FINAL BOOK, and in it is where I save the INTERIOR and COVER files for the paperback version, and another new folder called EBOOK where I save the final "INTERIOR EBOOK- My Book Title" ebook file and the "COVER EBOOK - My Book Title.jpg" file used for the ebook cover.

A little organization up front goes a long way.

You don't have to use my system, but whatever system you do use, make sure you stick to it because things go wrong all the time, and knowing where you saved everything eases the publishing pains, especially when you're uploading your book to Amazon for the very first time.

WHAT IS BLEED?

Bleed is a printing term that essentially means whether or not images or graphics reach all the way to the edge of the page.

All book covers on KDP require bleed. However, you can choose whether your interior has bleed or not. For photobooks, calendars etc. you would want interiors with bleed (w/bleed) because you most likely do not want white around your images, whereas novels and most non-fiction books are typically set to 'No Bleed.

The page on the left below is with bleed (the image extends to the very edge of the page.) On the right is an example of "No Bleed" because the image is within the margins.

Part 6 –Pricing

Once you finished writing and editing your book and verified that the print version and the ebook version are formatted the way you want, the next step is to set up an account on KDP.

To do this, visit: kdp.amazon.com

Your KDP account is connected to and uses the same credentials as your Amazon customer account, and that is the login you will use to sign in to KDP.

Through your KDP account you manage your personal, bank, and tax information, and it's where you upload your manuscripts and covers to self-publish them as ebooks and paperbacks through KDP, and it's where you set the price and track your sales.

WHAT'S A GOOD PRICE?

Amazon will give you a minimum price you have to set your paperback to cover printing costs. To make a profit selling paperbacks, the price you charge must be higher than the printing costs. KDP will automatically show you how much profit you will make on each sale, and you can set different prices for different countries.

How much you charge for your book or ebook depends a lot on your research of other books in your niche, and how much profit you wish to make.

Keep in mind that if other ebooks in your niche similar in size to your ebook are selling for $2.99, pricing your book at $9.99 may 'scare people off' even if you think your book is more valuable and contains more relevant information.

Buyers don't know that and they most likely won't spend that much to find out! They only know that you're a lot more expensive than other authors in your niche (who most likely already have some reviews compared to your brand-new book that doesn't have any reviews yet.) You have to be competitive even if that means selling your book for a little less than you want.

On the flip side of the coin, **pricing your ebook too low can work against you.** If your competition is selling their ebooks for $9.99 and you price your ebook at the minimum 99 cents, potential buyers may believe that your ebook has less to offer, or that you don't believe in yourself enough to try and compete.

It's a weird situation… people are generally looking for the best price, but 'perceived value' also plays an important role. **You do not want to be the most expensive or the cheapest.**

Keep in mind also that just because your competition has their ebooks set at $2.99, $5.99 or whatever, **doesn't necessarily mean they are actually selling their ebooks at those prices**. Just like you used an online ASIN calculator to find profitable niches to write about, you use the same tools to look up your competition to see if they are actually selling their ebooks at those prices.

Too many first-time authors see that most ebooks in their niche are priced at the standard $2.99 so that's the price they choose, but in reality, no one is really getting a lot of sales at that price point.

The most profitable ebooks in that niche might actually be selling at 99 cents, $1.99, or maybe $5.99. You should always do a bit of research before setting your price if you wish to compete with the ebooks that are _actually_ selling.

If you enroll your ebook in 'KDP Select' (more on that in just a moment) you have to set your ebook at a minimum of $2.99; if other ebooks in your niche are selling at 99 cents or $1.99, you might be hurting your sales potential by being too expensive because you do not have the reviews yet to back up that higher price.

It's a game of give and take, and it sometimes requires a bit of experimenting to find what the best price point for your ebook is, not to mention some research. If you choose to use KDP select, you're automatically locked into a 3-month period and you cannot experiment with different prices.

Remember also that you should not change your price every other day to try and find the 'sweet spot' because it takes time, and a lot of self-promotion, for your book to gain traction anyway. So don't keep changing your prices willy-nilly hoping to find that magic number… research, time, and patience (and a lot of marketing) is how you find your perfect price.

EBOOK PRICING

To sell an ebook on Amazon it has to be a minimum of 99 cents, and you receive 30% of all sales.

But Kenn, earlier you said people used a hack to 'sell their books for free' to get listed as a best-selling author even though they didn't actually sell any books because they were giving them away. How is this possible if 99 cents is the minimum price?

Another hack people discovered is to first set their price at the minimum 99 cents, and then upload a copy of their ebook to Google Books (or somewhere else) and set that price as free. They would then contact Amazon and notify them that there is a cheaper price elsewhere, and Amazon would price match it and drop the price to $0.00. It does take a little while for Amazon to drop the price to free, but this hack is useful if you insist on giving your book away for free.

Just remember what I said about the perceived value people place on free stuff.

KDP SELECT

If you wish to enroll your ebook to the Kindle Select program, the minimum price is $2.99 (you receive 70% of all sales.) Amazon has plenty of helpfiles to explain the KDP Select program and how the pricing structure works.

It's worth noting that once you enroll your new ebook in KDP Select, you CANNOT publish your ebook anywhere else (such as Google Books, Smashwords, Apple eBook Store and others) for the first three months.

PRE-SELLING & INCREMENTING SALES

Another option you can use is pre-selling your ebook, and through KDP Select you can have incrementing sales, such as 99 cents for 1 week, then $1.99 for the second week, then finally it goes up to $2.99 (or whatever your 'regular price' is) from that point on.

The thought process behind this is called FOMO (Fear of Missing out) because people are more likely to purchase the book at a lower price because they know the price is going up soon and they don't want to miss out on the deal by hesitating.

I've never really benefited much from using the KDP Select program, so I don't use it anymore. It's a personal preference. **What you do, like everything else self-publishing, is entirely up to you**.

Most of the settings in KDP are fairly straight-forward. The more you use it, the easier it becomes to navigate the various options and, like everything else Amazon, they have tons of help files to explain everything you need to know.

Some people suggest marketing your book before it is actually available (or before you even write it) and to use the pre-order option. This is a good idea, but it comes with the following two caveats:

First, it puts you on a deadline. While some people strive under deadlines, others start to panic. The last thing you want to do is presell a book that you planned on releasing on a certain date, and then you missed your own deadline. The people who purchased your book will not like it; neither will Amazon.

The second is, if you decided to completely finish your book before choosing the pre-selling option just so you don't miss your deadline, I know how excited you will be that your book is done, and you'll want to share it with everyone to get the word out so they can read it because word-of-mouth referrals are the best way to sell books, but you can't really do that per se because you have to wait until the publishing date before they can read it. Most people don't have the patience for that and want to get the ball rolling as quickly as possible, especially first-time authors.

Yes, people can pre-order your book, but if you want people to be able to buy and read it right away, and if patience is not your strong suit, maybe just uploading it and skipping over the presales part is the way to go for you.

That's the way I do it because once my book is uploaded, I want to start promoting it. I don't want to 'sit on it' to use the presales options if the book is already finished, and I don't want to risk missing the deadline if I use presales before I finished the book because sometimes, life happens…

Any number of things can happen during that period that keeps you from finishing your book.

It's not worth the risk, especially for your first couple of books.

Once you have more experience writing, and you developed strong writing habits so you'll know exactly how long it will take you to finish your book, preselling is a great way to build hype before your book is available on the Amazon marketplace.

It's worth noting that if you do use preselling, having a number of people buy the book before it is even available increases your sales rank when it is officially launched, so that is something else to consider before deciding whether or not preselling is for you.

Part 7 - Final Thoughts

Once you've uploaded and verified everything, selected your price, and then pressed PUBLISH, it takes the team at Amazon anywhere from 24 to 72 hours to verify your book and place it in the Amazon Marketplace.

After that you sit back and collect your royalties.

Not really…

After you publish your book you start promoting it through your favorite social media platforms.

As I mentioned a few times: when it comes to self-publishing, how you do it is entirely up to you. Just remember that **Amazon does not promote your book (unless you pay for ads) so your sales are 99.9% dependant on your own book marketing efforts.**

There is a chance that some people will stumble upon your book and buy it, but if you want more than the odd random sale, that is, you want to create a second income, or use book publishing as your primary source of income, you have to do a lot of self-promotion.

Just remember what I said earlier: the more books you have available for sale, the more books you will sell. The chances of you being able to quit your day job and live off book royalties from one book are slim to none. You have a better chance of winning the lottery.

Yes, sometimes it does happen. J.K. Rowling is a great example of a super successful, first-time author who was rejected by publishers several times before one of them took a chance on her, but she is the exception to the rule, and she found a publisher. Most first-time indie authors only make a few bucks per month because they don't consistently promote their book, which often means paying for ads on places like Amazon, Facebook, or some other avenue, and they often only have the one book.

It takes money to make money.

Writing and publishing your book is the easy part; selling it will prove to be more difficult, and sometimes quite frustrating, but that's a topic for a future book.

If you want to create a second income or quit your day job and become a full-time writer, you must get serious about writing and publishing by constantly finding hot niches, writing and publishing as many quality books as you can that have great content, and building your name and brand by promoting the hell out of your books by using self-promotion, word of mouth, and paid advertising, all why writing and publishing new books in other hot niches.

Or… you can just write and sell books as a hobby.

The choice is yours.

Whichever path you choose, I wish you much success.

Now go write your book!

Kenn

A Simple Request

Thanks for reading this book. I sincerely hope it helps and inspires you to get your book idea out of your head and on the written page. I have one quick favor to ask...

If you enjoyed this book I'd be super grateful if you left an honest review about it on Amazon.

It'll mean the world to me because every single review counts.

Use the link below to leave a quick review on the book's Amazon page. Thanks so much for your kind support!

Cheers,
Kenn

Type this link into your browser to be taken directly to the review page:

kenncrawford.com/review_wpnf

OTHER BOOKS BY KENN CRAWFORD

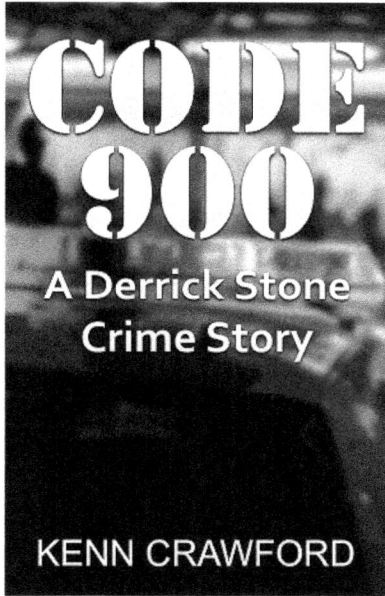

CODE 900
A Derrick Stone Crime Story
KENN CRAWFORD

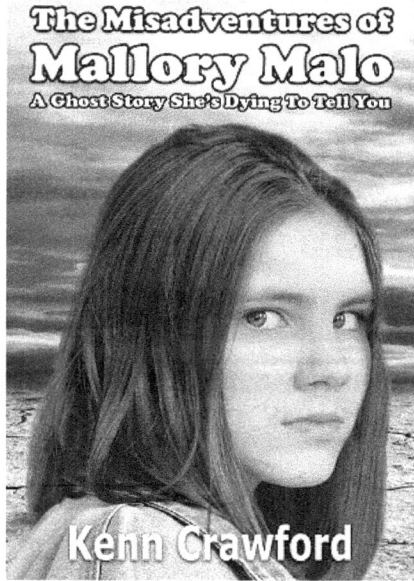

The Misadventures of **Mallory Malo**
A Ghost Story She's Dying To Tell You
Kenn Crawford

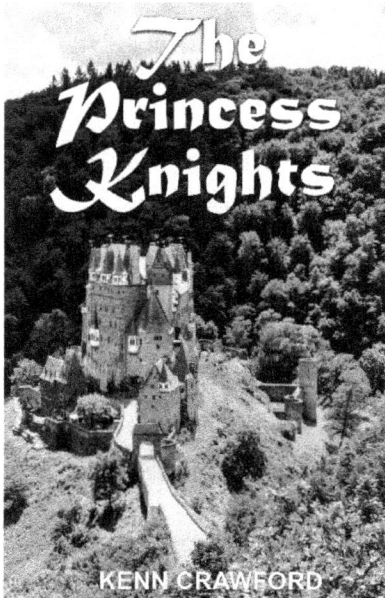

The Princess Knights
KENN CRAWFORD

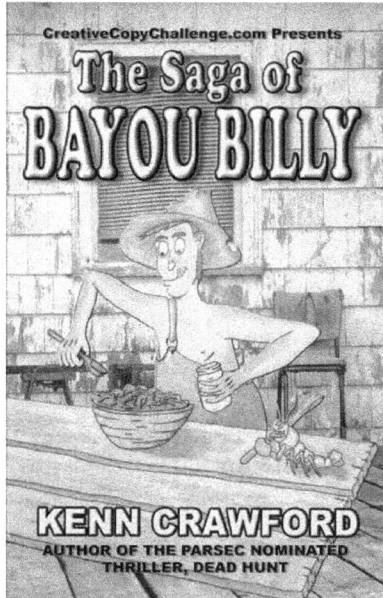

CreativeCopyChallenge.com Presents
The Saga of **BAYOU BILLY**
KENN CRAWFORD
AUTHOR OF THE PARSEC NOMINATED THRILLER, DEAD HUNT

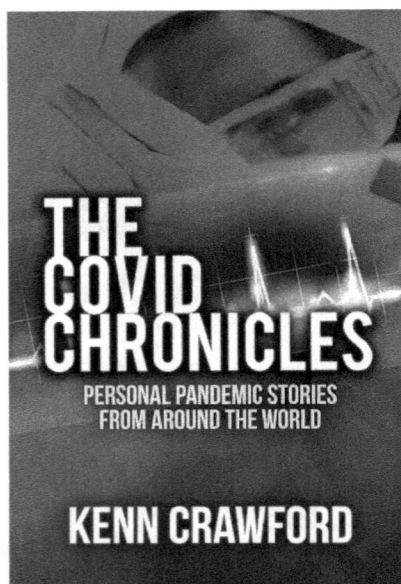

THE COVID CHRONICLES
PERSONAL PANDEMIC STORIES FROM AROUND THE WORLD
KENN CRAWFORD

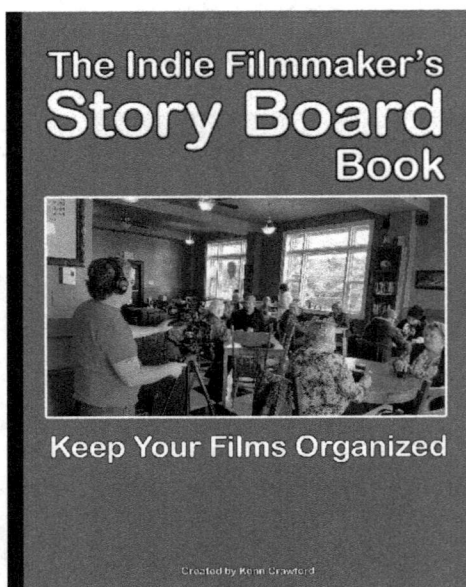

The Indie Filmmaker's
Story Board
Book
Keep Your Films Organized
Created by Kenn Crawford

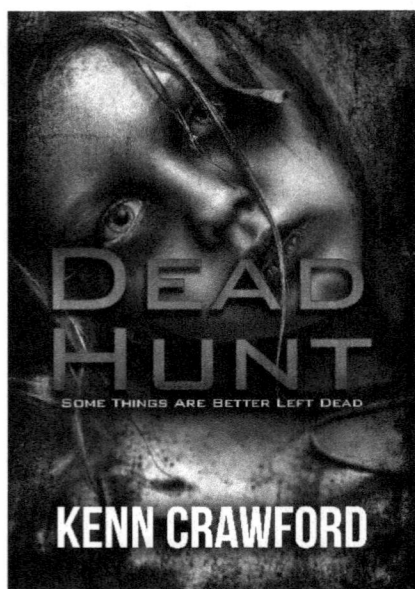

DEAD HUNT
SOME THINGS ARE BETTER LEFT DEAD
KENN CRAWFORD

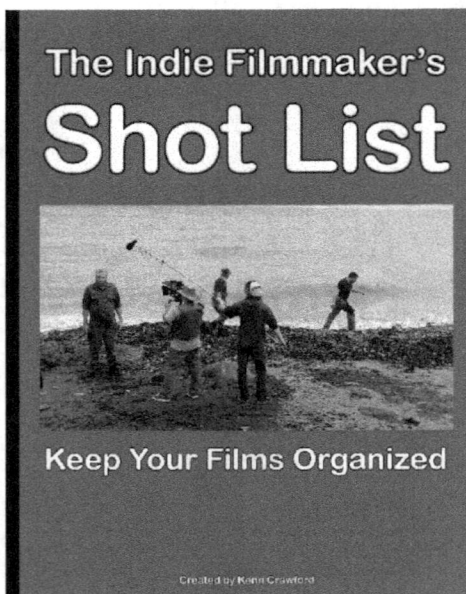

The Indie Filmmaker's
Shot List
Keep Your Films Organized
Created by Kenn Crawford

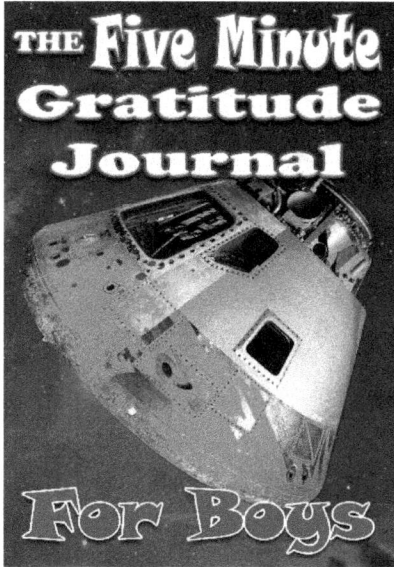

THE **Five Minute** Gratitude Journal For Boys

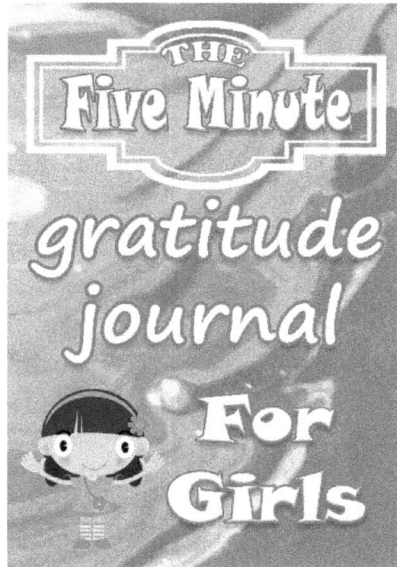

THE Five Minute gratitude journal For Girls

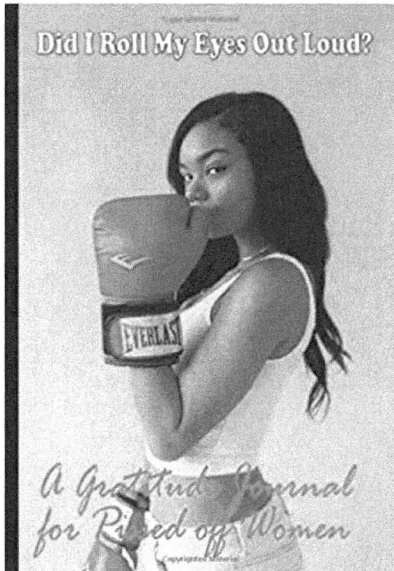

Did I Roll My Eyes Out Loud? A Gratitude Journal for Pissed off Women

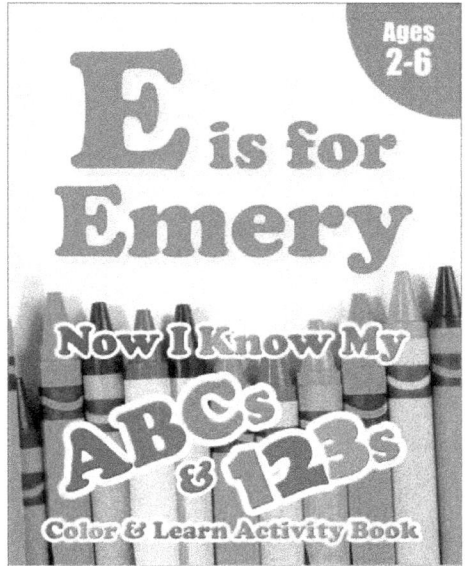

Ages 2-6 E is for Emery Now I Know My ABCs & 123s Color & Learn Activity Book

Novels & Novellas:
kenncrawford.com/books

Journals and Gratitude Journals: **kenncrawford.com/journals**

Personalized Children's Coloring Books:
kenncrawford.com/128page_coloringbook

www.ingramcontent.com/pod-product-compliance
Lightning Source LLC
Chambersburg PA
CBHW060320050426
42449CB00011B/2582